PRAYER

"Rev. John Clark Mayden, Jr.'s mastery of the metaphor is on full display as he teaches us how to connect with God and experience peace and wholeness through prayer. As a follow-up to his inspiring and uplifting work, *Breaking the Barriers: 31 Keys to Experience Inner Peace*, *Prayer: The Most Reliable Wireless Communication* is an inviting and intriguingly fun read through which he illuminates the enigma of prayer in contemporary language we all understand. Welcome to your next 'A-ha!' moment. This is therapy for the soul."

—Patricia L. Alfin, MSW
LCSW-Clinical, Retired

"Rev. John Clark Mayden, Jr. is a gifted and visionary leader. His ability to connect spiritual and practical insights is transformational. He brings to this resource experience and a forward looking view of how the spiritual discipline of prayer can be reincorporated into our busy routines. In a time when mindfulness, mediation, and other self-development disciplines are shaping helpful life habits, this resource uses Biblical wisdom to resource our lives in a meaningful way."

—Dr. Rodney Thomas Smothers
Director of Leadership and Congregational Development of Baltimore-Washington Conference/The United Methodist Church and Leadership Coach

PRAYER

THE MOST RELIABLE WIRELESS COMMUNICATION

REV. JOHN CLARK MAYDEN, JR.

Prayer
The Most Reliable Wireless Communication
©2020 by Rev. John Clark Mayden, Jr.
All rights reserved

ISBN: 978-1-62020-978-3
eISBN: 978-1-62020-992-9

Cover Design and Page Layout by Hannah Nichols
eBook Conversion by Anna Riebe Raats

No part of this book may be used or reproduced in any manner whatsoever without written permission except in the case of brief quotations embodied in critical articles or reviews.

Unless otherwise indicated, Bible quotations are taken from THE HOLY BIBLE, NEW INTERNATIONAL VERSION®, NIV® Copyright © 1973, 1978, 1984, 2011 by Biblica, Inc.® Used by permission. All rights reserved worldwide.

Scripture quotations marked MSG taken from THE MESSAGE, copyright © 1993, 1994, 1995, 1996, 2000, 2001, 2002 by Eugene H. Peterson. Used by permission of NavPress. All rights reserved. Represented by Tyndale House Publishers, Inc.

Scripture quotations marked NLT taken from the Holy Bible, New Living Translation, copyright © 1996, 2004, 2015 by Tyndale House Foundation. Used by permission of Tyndale House Publishers, Inc., Carol Stream, Illinois 60188. All rights reserved.

AMBASSADOR INTERNATIONAL
Emerald House
411 University Ridge, Suite B14
Greenville, SC 29601, USA
www.ambassador-international.com

AMBASSADOR BOOKS
The Mount
2 Woodstock Link
Belfast, BT6 8DD, Northern Ireland, UK
www.ambassadormedia.co.uk

The colophon is a trademark of Ambassador, a Christian publishing company.

This book is dedicated to my Lord and Savior Jesus Christ and my wife, Kirstyn, daughter, Naomi, and my family, and is written to help readers to pursue God in prayer.

CONTENTS

PREFACE 9

CHAPTER 1
THE OLDEST FORM OF WIRELESS COMMUNICATION 13

CHAPTER 2
CHARGING MY DEVICE 19

CHAPTER 3
WIRELESS DEVICES 25

CHAPTER 4
POWERING ON 33

CHAPTER 5
THE MOST RELIABLE WIRELESS COMMUNICATION 39

CHAPTER 6
7 KEYS TO EXPERIENCING GOD'S PRESENCE AND POWER 55

CHAPTER 7
PRAYER AND HEALTH 85

CHAPTER 8
LOCKED OUT   101

CHAPTER 9
BUILDING A STRONGER NETWORK   111

CONCLUSION   121

AFTERWORD   123

BIBLIOGRAPHY   125

ACKNOWLEDGMENTS   129

PREFACE

The advent of wireless communication has been a game changer in North America and the United Kingdom. People no longer depend on wires to communicate with other people. Gone are the days of payphones, slow dial-up connections, and the large, heavy desktop machines. The click of a button allows people to connect locally and abroad. Now, we live in an age where faster mobile technology has caught on like wildfire.

Prayer, the oldest form of wireless communication, is uttered before meals, at bedtime, and during worship services. One expresses gratitude, cries, burdens, and moans in a language called prayer. The influence of prayer is widespread and is practiced in every world religion because every faith tradition views prayer as sacred. Recognizing the global impact of prayer, I will use as my primary references the Judeo-Christian prayer for examples from the Old and New Testaments. Readers will also find examples from other religious traditions to emphasize the universal recognition of prayer as a necessity in the lives of humanity.

The Hebrew word for *pray* is "tefilah," which means to "beg, beseech and implore." The Jewish prophets of the Old Testament begged and prayed to God. For our purposes, prayer is to help attach us to God and purify our hearts. This is seen in The New Living Translation's version of Psalm 51:9: "Don't keep looking at my sins. Remove the stain of my guilt." The central theme found in this passage is purification of the heart.

The Greek (New Testament language) verb *proseuchomai* means "to pray." The first part of the word, *pros,* means "towards and exchange." Throughout the pages of the New Testament, *pros* highlight a connection or contact between people. The second part of the word, which is *euchomai*, means "to wish, pray."[1] Initially, during the New Testament times, people would make a vow to God because they had a desire or a need. Their goal was to have their needs met by God through prayer.

WHAT IS PRAYER?

Most of the time, I find prayer to be a monologue and not a two-way conversation. If we pay attention to our prayers, we will notice that we are directing our requests to God without expecting a verbal response. We just wish to voice whatever is on our hearts and minds, hoping that God hears us. In fact, thumbing through the pages of the Bible, I realize that most prayers offered by humans are one-sided. But what is prayer?

The Holy Scriptures provide us with some helpful definitions for prayer. Prayer is calling on God. In Jeremiah 33:3, God urges the Hebrew prophet Jeremiah to call on the name of the Lord in times of trouble. An accepted definition of the term *call* means to speak out loud. Therefore, Jeremiah informs us that prayer is inviting God to come into a situation or circumstance. To paint a clear picture, Jeremiah cried out to God during the physical exile of the Jewish people from their homeland of Judah. The Babylonians conquered the Israelites; and amid immense suffering, Jeremiah urged the people to call on the Lord.

Christian author and theologian Timothy Keller identifies that "prayer is a personal, communicative response to the knowledge of God."[2] In other words, prayer is recognizing that we don't have all the answers and solutions to our situations and that we need the help of God in our lives. Another way of putting this is that God is the One Who fills in the gaps in our lives. For

---

1 *Bible Hub*, s.v. "proseuchomai," accessed on June 4, 2018, http://biblehub.com/greek/4336.htm.
2 Timothy Keller, *Prayer: Experiencing Awe and Intimacy with God*, New York, NY: Penguin Books, 2014, p. 45.

example, I pray that I lose weight, but I must exercise to achieve the goal. This demonstrates the work that accompanies prayer.

Renowned Quaker scholar and author Richard Foster states, "Prayer is the human response to the perpetual outpouring of love by which God lays siege to every soul."[3] This means that God's glorious blessings and intervention in our lives initiates the action of prayer. We pray because of God's goodness. Throughout my book, I will borrow the terminology from Richard Foster's book to describe prayer in three movements: outward, inward, and upward.

These definitions help us make the determination that prayer is a lifestyle. It is important to understand that prayer is not a momentary practice but an extension of one's life because prayer must be accompanied by action. It dictates one's decision-making.

THE PURPOSE OF THIS BOOK

Prayer: The Most Reliable Wireless Communication is a contemporary commentary written to speak about the ancient practice of prayer in a new way. Using wireless terminology as an illustration, I aim to provide fresh insights for prayer. Hopefully, this practical resource will assist you in your quest to effectively communicate with God. Be prepared to experience a greater depth of God's presence and power and a renewed assurance that your prayers matter.

SCRIPTURAL REFERENCES

The Scriptures are a key source for my work. The New International Version will be my primary scriptural reference. With that said, the original biblical languages of Hebrew (Old Testament) and koine Greek (Hellenistic Greek found in the New Testament) will be used to help covey the meaning

---

[3] Richard Foster, *Prayer: The Hearts True Home*, San Francisco, CA: Harper One, 2002, p. 85.

of some of the terms of my book. Though Aramaic is also an original biblical language in the Hebrew Bible, for the purposes of this book, I will not use Aramaic in this writing.

INSPIRATION

The idea for this manuscript was conceived in 2007 during a sermon entitled "Prayer the Best Wireless Communication," presented at the historic John Wesley United Methodist Church, located in Baltimore, Maryland. As I sat on those hard, wooden pews, I recall hearing the Spirit of God instruct me to devote time and attention to the topic of prayer in the form of a book. After listening and digesting the great depth of the sermon, I learned and developed new insights and an approach to prayer that I wanted to share with others.

CHAPTER 1

THE OLDEST FORM OF WIRELESS COMMUNICATION

But the Lord God *called to the man, "Where are you?"* (Genesis 3:9).

The earliest recorded prayers are traced to Hinduism, the oldest known world religion founded in 2300 BCE (Before Common Era).[4] These prayers are said to be between six thousand to seven thousand years old.[5] These prayers are chants and have poetic and ritualistic meaning.

In ancient Hinduism, prayer was viewed as transcendent. It provided space for one to connect with the divine or their own self in a spiritual way. The prayer philosophy of this faith is that one will experience freedom as his or her thoughts are placed on the divine because worries and fears will begin to dissipate. Below is a Hindu prayer:

> "Earth in which the seas, the rivers and many waters lie, from which arise foods and fields of grain, abode to all that breathes and moves, may She confer on us Her finest yield."[6]

There is a rhythmic flow to this holistic prayer. Nature is the content of this prayer. Finally, we get a glimpse of the Hindu theology which highlights the dominion of the divine over creation.

---

4 "Hinduism Fast Facts," CNN.com, https://www.cnn.com/2013/11/07/world/hinduism-fast-facts/index.html (accessed on August 7, 2019).
5 Jayaram V., "A Few Thoughts About Prayers in Hinduism,"HinduWebsite.com, https://www.hinduwebsite.com/ask/how-to-pray.asp (accessed on April 20, 2019).
6 Bhumi Suktam, Atharva Veda xii.1.3 (accessed on August 5, 2019).

PRAYER IN THE BIBLE

The first recorded prayer in the Hebrew Bible (also known as the Old Testament) comes to us in Genesis 3:9-13. Biblical scholarship dates the book of Genesis back to 1445 BC (Before Christ).[7] This prayer is over thirty-four hundred years old and features God confronting Adam and Eve for partaking of the forbidden fruit. In addition, Adam and Eve provide excuses for their disobedience.

> But the Lord God called to the man, "Where are you?" He answered, "I heard you in the garden, and I was afraid because I was naked; so I hid." And he said, "Who told you that you were naked? Have you eaten from the tree that I commanded you not to eat from?" The man said, "The woman you put here with me—she gave me some fruit from the tree, and I ate it." Then the Lord God said to the woman, "What is this you have done?" The woman said, "The serpent deceived me, and I ate" (Genesis 3:9-13).

We see from this example that prayer is depicted as a two-way conversation with God. In this chat, God questioned Adam and Eve about their disobedience, and they had excuses. Notice the passage doesn't mention God speaking to Adam and Eve through a device with wires. It is just communication that occurred with no strings attached.

It appears that Adam and Eve were straightforward with God. He shared the account of what transpired between him and his wife, which convinced him to get to the forbidden fruit. By no means is this a defense of Adam's action, but both Adam and Eve told God what happened. This was heartfelt and honest communication.

The practical aspect of Adam's prayer that we may apply to our prayer life is that giving a recount in what is happening in your life is an excellent prayer starter. We don't have to beat around the bush with God but should tell

---
7 "Bible Summary Table," BibleAnswers.study, https://bibleanswers.study/bible-summary-table (accessed on August 5, 2019).

God what is happening in our day. When it comes to prayer, we should share everything with God.

There are numerous recorded prayers in the Old Testament. The book of Psalms contains many of these prayers. During antiquity, many of these prayers were recited in the worship services.

Within the New Testament, we also find recorded prayers. The one that I will highlight in this chapter is the Lord's Prayer. In the first two decades of the first century AD (Anno Domini), Jesus taught His disciples how to pray using this prayer as a model. This familiar prayer is uttered in worship services and homes throughout the globe. It is found in two Gospels (Matthew 6:9-13 and Luke 11:2-4). I will use Luke's version:

> He said to them, "When you pray, say:
>
> "'Father, hallowed be your name, your kingdom come. Give us each day our daily bread. Forgive us our sins, for we also forgive everyone who sins against us. And lead us not into temptation.'"

This prayer is vast and covers a lot of ground. Reverencing God, forgiveness and overcoming temptation are all mentioned in this groundbreaking prayer. The subject matter found in this prayer should guide us in our everyday prayers.

Now, I will take a slight turn and discuss the overall premise and purpose behind prayer in different religious traditions. Looking at the purpose of prayer in Eastern and Western religions will help us gain a comprehensive perspective on prayer through the centuries. Understanding the thought process of prayer by the ancients will help us comprehend why prayer is necessary and meaningful in our lives.

PRAYER IN EASTERN RELIGIONS

In the Eastern Asian religions of Hinduism and Buddhism, prayer is a means to heighten one's awareness of the presence of the divine. (Though

Jainism and Sikhism are Eastern Asian religions, I will not discuss these faith traditions in this work). In Hinduism, prayer draws us into contact with our personality; as we explore our intentions we reach a higher level of consciousness. Buddhism views prayer as unselfish and centers on human kindness as opposed to worldly gain. The goal is to mend human brokenness through love. Fruits of prayer are sharing, generosity, and renewed purpose.

I want to provide some more information about a higher level of consciousness. A higher level of consciousness highlights that humans should serve a greater power than self. This renewed mindset helps people get beyond their ego and selfish desires. A higher level of consciousness means caring about other individuals more than oneself. This consciousness improves the overall well-being of humanity. An example of this is serving the poor without seeking a reward.

PRAYER IN WESTERN RELIGIONS

In Western religions—such as Judaism, Christianity, and Islam—prayer is viewed as a source of healing, transformation, reconciliation, and deliverance. It is something that is a change agent and leads to situational change and personal and spiritual growth through God. Within these religions, prayer takes on three relational aspects: Inwardly, prayer gives us clarity about our purpose, which deals with sharpening our mental, physical, and emotional capacities for the ups and downs of life. Upwardly, we seek to grow closer and develop a more intimate relationship with the Maker. Outwardly, we want the lives and situations of others to improve. These movements emphasize the process and shape that prayer takes.

Both Eastern and Western Religions view prayer as sacred and incorporate this practice into their daily routines. This act of worship helps people take their eyes and attention off self and place it on the divine. Change is often a result of sincere prayer.

WHY DID PEOPLE IN THE BIBLE PRAY?

Historically, in the Old Testament, Jewish people turned to the Most High for help (Psalm 54:4), safety (Psalm 11:1), punishment of their enemies (Psalm 137), and protection (Psalm 91:1-2). They sought God out of necessity. They realized that situations came their way that they couldn't handle, and they understood that God is the One Who can handle their circumstances.

Psalm 61:2 epitomizes the supremacy of God and the need to pray. While King David flees his enemies, he takes time to acknowledge God as the Rock. Psalm 61:2 says, "From the ends of the earth I call to you, I call as my heart grows faint; lead me to the rock that is higher than I." Referring to God as "the Rock that is higher than I" means that God is the One Who is above David and his issues and the One he needs.

In the New Testament, the early believers prayed for breakthroughs in the lives of humanity. They prayed for the salvation of others (Romans 10:1), healing (Matthew 9:27-30), discipleship (John 17:6-26), unity (John 17), and deliverance (Mark 5:1-20).

The above paragraphs emphasized what prayer does. Now, we will dive into the reason for prayer.

WHY PRAY?

Humanity desperately needs God. Just look at the numerous social problems throughout civilization. Senseless gun violence claims the lives of innocent boys, girls, men, and women every day in the world. There are diseases—such as the Zika virus, cancer, and diabetes—where there is no identifiable cure. Global poverty seems like an impossible issue to address. In North America and in the U.K., the middle class is rapidly shrinking. Racially charged hate crimes continue to occur. Terrorist attacks rage throughout the world. In response to these and many other challenges, the writer of the Book of James tells us that when we endure hardships, we should pray (James 5:13).

We need to look for God amid these social ills for healing and radical change. These are all reasons to pray for situations and for circumstances to turn around in a positive direction by the work of God.

The above pressing conditions lead people to pray, but I also want to look at a variety of other reasons that people pray. Understanding the why of prayer highlights the goal of prayer. People pray to seek answers to their dilemmas: handling financial challenges, overcoming addiction, maintaining employment, looking for a mate, repairing a broken marriage, and even seeking a win for their favorite sports team. In every case, people pray to seek support in an area of life that is of significance to them. From the onset of this book, I want to make it clear that prayer is the vehicle that God uses to deliver power to individuals and the world. It is important to note that prayer itself is not powerful, but God is the Power Source.

To be clear, we shouldn't just pray during times of trouble. In fact, one establishes and maintains a relationship with the living God through prayer. Jesus continued to pray during His earthly ministry—such as before He walked on water (Matthew 14:23) and choosing the twelve disciples (Luke 6:12-13). Daily contact and sharing take place through this sacred act.

Prayer has been used for many purposes. Religious traditions and philosophies dictate the reasons for prayer. Though prayer is ancient; it remains relevant. People have prayed for years and continue to be amazed at the work of God in their lives.

CHAPTER 2
CHARGING MY DEVICE

"Come to me, all you who are weary and burdened, and I will give you rest" (Matthew 11:28).

One is unable to use his or her device if the device is not charged. This means that one can't do any work on the device such as email, send text messages or work on a Word document if there is not enough battery life on the device. Charging the device is essential to providing power to the device, and for the record, a cord or charger is needed to charge an electronic device.

When devices are not charged, the screen may become dim. An individual may be in the process of typing an email or a text message, but is interrupted by the screen going black. This is distracting and disrupting.

Like an uncharged device impacts service, prayerlessness affects a person. Prayerlessness may be a factor for the dimness that people experience in their lives. They may feel a void in their lives because of a disconnection with God. Just like a device needs to be charged to operate; we need to be connected to God through prayer to commune with our Creator.

THE NEED TO BE CHARGED

All the demands and stressors in life—school, work and social demands—often drain us. Our daily tasks are taxing and overwhelm our bodies, wearing us down. During these moments, we need to be charged. The question is how do we get charged?

Our lives need to be charged daily by God through prayer. God charges us by preparing and equipping us for the day. The charge that I am referring to is a spiritual charge, which will also manifest itself emotionally and physically. A spiritual charge gives us energy, and this charge will help in all areas and aspects of life. For example, one may deal with discouragement and need a jolt of encouragement from the Lord. It represents an energy and confidence boost. In other words, prayer helps and guides us. Prayer brings life, hope, and energy to our lives. Look at the apostle Paul, tormented by a thorn in his flesh, which would not go away (2 Corinthians 12:6-8). This thorn was annoying and could have served as a distraction from him doing what God called him to do. He prayed for his healing so that he would be charged for the ministry that God had for him to do.

Being charged involves resting in the Lord. This means not allowing circumstances to trouble us. Chaos and confusion may surround us, but do not have to negatively affect us. Think about when you are in a deep sleep. There may be external noises around you, but you are not awakened by those noises. These noises are not disrupting your sleep. Resting in the Lord means that our comfort and confidence completely reside in God so that no matter what is going on around us we may have peace.

HOW CAN I CHARGE?

You may be sitting there thinking that it sounds as though a charge is what you need, but how do you charge yourself in prayer? The charge comes through taking some alone time with God. In other words, take a break from the things that require your attention. Give yourself permission to take a break from working, doing household tasks, studying, and ministering to focus on God through prayer.

After immense testing by the devil in Matthew 4 and the Sermon on the Mount in Matthew 5, Jesus is seen being charged through the Lord's Prayer in Matthew 6. After reciting this prayer, Jesus receives miraculous power for the healing and restorative ministry that awaited Him—healing the sick (Matthew 8:3), restoring sight to the blind (Matthew 9:27-30), causing the dumb to talk (Matthew 15:31), removing demonic possessions (Matthew 8:28-34), and raising people from the dead (Matthew 8:17). For Jesus to minister to the needy, He needed to be emotionally stable and secure, and prayer aided Him in those areas.

In everyday life, charging deals with self-care. We need to take care of ourselves through resting. A way to do this is to take a personal Sabbath. During this Sabbath, turn the cell phone off and disconnect from the busyness of life. These actions will help us to take care of ourselves. We will be able to rest and focus on ourselves. As we rest, our bodies will be renewed and strengthened for the journey of life.

PERSISTENT PRAYER

"Pray continually" (1 Thessalonians 5:17).

Persistence is vital during the charging and reenergizing process. In the technology realm; mobile users will try to locate outlets to charge their devices. I have observed persistence in people that have a dying battery attempt to identify a power source so that their battery could be charged. Last week, I observed a lady ask the instructor of her class; if she could use the wall outlet to charge her phone. This individual persisted until she found an outlet to charge her phone. She easily could have allowed her cell phone battery to die and wait until she returned to a familiar environment to charge her phone, but she persisted.

Like the persistence needed in operating wireless devices, we need to be persistent in pursuing God to a greater extent. That is what it means in

James 5:16 when it says, "The prayer of a righteous person is powerful and effective." You need to continue to seek Him no matter what is going on in your life.

Persistent prayer also keeps the lines of communication open between us and God. This persistent prayer will keep us connected with the Lord. Think about it this way: If we immediately received what we asked God for, we would probably not continue to pray. Instead, persistent prayer is like running a marathon. We must continue to run (pray) to get to the finish line (our death).

With prayer, we must continue to pray, whether we receive the desired result or not. Our praying should not be contingent on our feelings. We should not stop praying because we don't like the way a situation is going. When we do this, we throw in the towel.

Thinking about persistence reminds me of when I was a little boy. As a little boy, I wanted to open a gift on Christmas Eve. I continued to make this request known to my parents. They reminded me of our family tradition, which is to open all Christmas gifts on Christmas day. Their response to me did not stop me from continuing to ask to open the gift a day early. Finally, my parents decided to allow me to open one present on Christmas Eve, so I got my way because of my persistence.

Do you want change in your life? Keep on praying. Persistent prayer is like the necessity of water to human and animal survival; we need it to survive.

James 5:17-18 provides us an account of persistent prayer as it recounts 1 Kings 18:41-46. Persistent prayer comes to the forefront in the life of the Hebrew prophet Elijah. In verse forty-three, Elijah prays on the heels of a brutal execution of 450 Baal prophets. These prophets pushed for the worship of Baal, a Philistine god. So, Elijah prayed for the purification of the land from idolatry in verses thirty-six and thirty-seven. The idolatry came into the land because of King Ahab, the king of Israel, and his wife, Jezebel.

Their idolatry and Baal worship caused a major drought in the land. The lack of rain was to get the attention of the Israelites and to help them turn to God.

An additional point that should help us be persistent in prayer is that God hears all prayer that is aligned with God's will. I am reminded of the words found in 1 John 5:14-15: "This is the confidence we have in approaching God: that if we ask anything according to his will, he hears us. And if we know that he hears us—whatever we ask—we know that we have what we asked of him." The point is that God hearing our prayers gives us the encouragement that we need to continue to pray.

A persistent prayer is something that may unfold over time. One example is my persistent prayer in my journey toward becoming a pastor. I received my call to preach at the age of fourteen years old and yet did not become a pastor until I was thirty-one years old. It took me seventeen years to achieve my goal and walk in my calling. The key is that I had to keep on praying.

LIVING OUT OUR PRAYER

Prayer that is persistent is lived out through our lifestyle. I lived out my persistent prayer by going through a series of events. Living out this prayer took me to several churches. It took me through multiple denominations. It took me through ordination examinations and discernment. It took me through restless nights. Ultimately, it kept my eyes and ears open to the Lord. This process involved praying and reading and studying Scriptures, which confirmed my calling. It involved constant prayer.

No matter what circumstance we find ourselves in, we need to pray. We need to pray when things aren't going our way. We need to pray when our health is failing. We need to pray when our children seem out of control. We need to pray when trouble comes our way.

Living out our prayer is the key to persistent prayer. This means taking the steps necessary for our request to come into being. We must continue to seek the Lord in all matters.

In conclusion, prayer charges us for the tasks of life. Strength and cautious decision-making will accompany us through prayer. A renewal of our minds and bodies will continue to take place in our lives with prayer. Today, please take the time to be charged by prayer.

CHAPTER 3
WIRELESS DEVICES

"In the last days, God says, I will pour out my Spirit on all people. Your sons and daughters will prophesy, your young men will see visions, your old men will dream dreams" (Acts 2:17).

THE PRIVILEGE OF WIRELESS COMMUNICATION

To own a wireless device is a privilege. The cost of a cell phone, tablet or a laptop can be expensive which means that everyone that wants to own one cannot afford to. Additionally, some parents will not purchase a cell phone, a tablet, or a laptop computer for their children until the child (ren) show that they are responsible. In other words, the children may have to earn good grades in school or complete their chores for a period of time. The point that parents are making to their child(ren) is that owning a wireless device is a privilege. This is not something that the child is entitled to, but instead must earn.

THE PRIVILEGE OF PRAYER

In the same vein, equally as important as persistently praying, we must realize that prayer is a privilege. It is something that should not be taken for granted. It is a blessing that we can pray. The reason that the infinite God decides to take time to be with the finite human is something that we are unable to explain. In fact, this is a mystery. With every prayer, we can petition the

Maker of the universe and ask for God's service. We should be grateful that God is not like a disengaged parent who does not heed to the cries of his or her children, but that God listens and answers our prayers. The Lord's Prayer is an amazing prayer in the Bible, underlining the privilege of prayer because we hear the regard that Jesus (the Son of God) holds toward His Father. Let's look at the first two words of this tremendous prayer.

The prayer opens with "Our Father," which conveys that God is a relational Being. We get a sense that Jesus is close to God. The fact that Jesus calls the Creator of all "Father" is incredible because it demonstrates the interpersonal nature of God. It is okay for a human to have this type of bond with the Architect of Creation. Clearly, there is an established relationship between the two, which demonstrates that there can be an open line of communication with God.

These opening words of this familiar prayer are like having a signal so that people can communicate using smartphones or any mobile device. The signal signifies that the smartphone user has service in an area. From a practical perspective, Jesus makes the statement that God is not distant but is a very close, heavenly Parent, who cares immensely for His Son.

For us, we can be assured that God is present during our most trying times and through the good times. This presence should serve as a source of comfort and serenity. Therefore, we can go through difficulties with confidence that we are not alone.

Prayer is not manipulation. We are not able to control God. However, prayer may stimulate God to act on our behalf. Persistent prayer does not mean that things change overnight, but you can continue to pray that they will. Things will shift when God allows these changes to take place.

Understanding the privilege of prayer may spark our curiosity about prayer. You may be thinking how does God communicate with humanity? The question may arise because communication is two-sided. The answer is that God communicates with humanity through the following wireless devices: visions, dreams, godly counsel, preaching, and Scripture. In other words, the Bible reveals that historically, God spoke to humanity through these six mediums.

VISIONS

Acts 11 provides us with a classic example of God responding to Peter's prayer with a vision. Peter was a man of God who wanted to spread the Gospel message. In this story, God revealed his mission for the Gospel to be spread to the Gentiles (non-Jews). We find Peter enlightened through his encounter with God in Acts 11:5-10, 17-18:

> "I was in the city of Joppa praying, and in a trance I saw a vision. I saw something like a large sheet being let down from heaven by its four corners, and it came down to where I was. I looked into it and saw four-footed animals of the earth, wild beasts, reptiles and birds. Then I heard a voice telling me, 'Get up, Peter. Kill and eat.' "I replied, 'Surely not, Lord! Nothing impure or unclean has ever entered my mouth.' "The voice spoke from heaven a second time, 'Do not call anything impure that God has made clean.' This happened three times, and then it was all pulled up to heaven again." So if God gave them the same gift he gave us who believed in the Lord Jesus Christ, who was I to think that I could stand in God's way?" When they heard this, they had no further objections and praised God, saying, "So then, even to Gentiles God has granted repentance that leads to life."

A vision is a forecast for a future event. God presents a picture to an individual of what is going to happen. These visions help us understand God's perspective and give us understanding on how to follow God's will. So, clearly, it was the will of God for the Gentiles to receive salvation. After receiving this vision, Peter understood and accepted God's inclusive view of salvation.

In 2017, the Lord gave me a vision for a community health fair that would take place in 2018. I envisioned an outdoor event with vendors providing community resources and services to residents in the area of our church. I visualized people growing in Christ and taking better care of themselves during this fun event. Through this vision, God provided me a foretaste of how the church will serve the community.

Visions provide us with a glimpse of what God has in store for us and other people. They provide a roadmap as to how God plans to impact humanity and the world. Keep your eyes open for visions that are from God.

DREAMS

Dreams are another way that the Lord communicates with us. Have you ever had a dream that you knew was from God? If so, you are not alone. Throughout the Scriptures, there are examples of people receiving dreams from God. A familiar biblical reference on dreams is when the prophet Daniel reveals the dream to King Nebuchadnezzar in Daniel 7. Daniel highlights the four successive kingdoms, which pale in comparison to the eternal Kingdom of God. In other words, the dream illustrates the superiority of God's Kingdom over the kingdoms of the Earth.

Thousands of years after King Nebuchadnezzar's dream, the late Rev. Dr. Martin Luther King, Jr., civil rights icon, delivered one of his most memorable speeches, entitled "I Have a Dream." This soul-stirring speech revealed to America and the rest of the world Dr. King's dream of racial equality for people of color, job opportunities for all individuals, and unity. I believe this dream was revealed to him from God in his Kitchen Table experience in 1956. Here's an excerpt from this extraordinary speech: "I have a dream that my four little children will one day live in a nation where they will not be judged by the color of their skin, but by the content of their character."[8] His speech seems in perfect alignment with Galatians 3:28, which declares, "There is neither Jew nor Gentile, neither

---
8 Martin Luther King, Jr., "I Have a Dream." Speech. Lincoln Memorial, Washington, D. C., August 28, 1963, American Rhetoric, Web (accessed on August 6, 2019).

slave nor free, nor is there male and female, for you are all one in Christ Jesus." This passage means that there is no superior race or class of people, but we are unified in Christ. Many people shared Dr. King's dream and dedicated themselves to making it a reality; it has transformed America and the world.

There is a final point that I need to make about dreams. Pay attention to your dreams that are related to God's Word. This means that God is relaying an important message to you.

PROPHETS

In the Bible, God spoke to people through prophets. In the Old Testament, the prophet would declare the Word of God to people. There were different types of prophets. Unfavorable prophets were Jeremiah and Isaiah, who proclaimed messages of doom and gloom to the Israelites. I call them unfavorable because some who listened to them probably didn't like them because of their message. Jeremiah prophesied the fall of Jerusalem (Jeremiah 6:2-4), and Isaiah prophesied the fall of Judah (2 Kings 20:12-21) because these are the messages they received from God. They made these bold assertions because of the sin of idolatry in the lands of Jerusalem and Judah. The people of that day didn't want to hear that they were living a sinful lifestyle. Yet, the prophets told the truth knowing that it would offend the listeners.

These prophets boldly spoke a Word from the Lord to the Jewish people. Notice in Jeremiah 1:4-10, God called and commissioned Jeremiah to be a prophet. It is here that God groomed Jeremiah to proclaim the truth to the Jewish people (Jeremiah 1:7). Isaiah 6:9 says that God said to Isaiah, "Go, and tell this people: 'Be ever hearing, but never understanding; be ever seeing, but never perceiving.'" This is when he was told that he would be a spokesman for God.

PREACHERS

Today, preachers speak a Word of God to people. On this point, Romans 10:14-15 tells us, "How, then, can they call on the one they have not believed in? And how can they believe in the one of whom they have not heard? And how can they hear without someone preaching to them? And how can anyone preach unless they are sent? As it is written: 'How beautiful are the feet of those who bring good news!'" God sends preachers to proclaim a powerful message to inspire and encourage the congregation to transform their lives.

Just as God spoke through the prophets in biblical times, God speaks today through preachers to their congregations. First Thessalonians 2:13 says, "And we also thank God continually because, when you received the word of God, which you heard from us, you accepted it not as a human word, but as it actually is, the word of God, which is indeed at work in you who believe." Every week, preachers proclaim the unadulterated Word of God to their congregation. Sometimes, these preachers address concerns and issues that their congregants have laid out at the altar to the Lord. During these times, the light bulb may go on in the head of a congregant, and they may understand something that God intends for them.

Listen to preachers whose messages are aligned with the Word of God. God will continue to speak through these men and women to proclaim messages of hope, love, and salvation. Be sure to have open ears and an open heart to receive the Word of the Lord.

GODLY COUNSEL

Another way to hear from God is through seeking Godly counsel. Proverbs 19:20 says, "Listen to advice and accept discipline, and at the end you will be counted among the wise." Seeking godly counsel means that we consult people who know God and have a relationship with God. I wouldn't go to an eye doctor about an automobile issue. Seeking godly counsel comes into play because an individual needs spiritual wisdom to deal with spiritual situations.

Throughout the Gospels, the disciples went to Jesus when they had questions about their inability to heal (Matthew 17:16). As a result of not being able to heal the boy with the seizures, they asked Jesus, "Why are we unable to heal this boy?" Jesus pointedly told them it was because of their lack of faith (Matthew 17:20). In this instance, they actively sought out the Lord because of their helplessness to address the situation.

I would be remiss not to mention that God also speaks to Christian believers through non-believers. Sometimes, God sends messengers through unlikely sources. For instance, Pharaoh told Moses and Aaron to get out of Egypt, which is what God intended (Exodus 3:10; 12:31). Pharaoh wasn't a man of faith at this time but reminds Moses and Aaron of their assignment from God, which is to get the Israelites out of Egypt.

SCRIPTURE

Additionally, God communicates through Scriptures. The Word of God is living and active (Hebrews 4:12). The Bible contains the answers to the questions of life. How should we interact with those around us? We are told to "love your neighbor as yourself" (Mark 12:31). When we feel mentally tired, we need to look at Matthew 11:28. How do we deal with emotional weight? "Come to me, all you who are weary and burdened, and I will give you rest." This means that God still speaks to us and our circumstances and this is an ongoing promise from God. When we feel anxious, how do we deal with anxiety? We find instructions in Isaiah 43:1: "But now, this is what the Lord says ... 'Do not fear, for I have redeemed you; I have summoned you by name; you are mine.'" These are just a couple of examples that point out that God speaks to our feelings and gives us hope.

SILENCE

There is a saying that silence is golden. The truth is that silence is also a means that God uses to speak to humanity. First Kings 19:11-13 gives an account of Elijah seeking the voice of God. "And after the earthquake a fire, but the LORD was not in the fire; and after the fire a sound of sheer silence." Silence is what God used to speak to Elijah in the middle of his difficulties.

Silence puts us in a position to receive from God what the Lord wants us to receive. We can disconnect from the noise of life. We can disconnect from the distractions. We can disconnect from negativity all around us.

By no means are these the only ways that God speaks to humanity. Yet, these are ways that I find in the Scriptures and have experienced personally: visions, dreams, prophets, preachers, godly counsel, Scripture, and even silence. These are all mediums that the Lord uses to convey important messages and tasks for us to do. Often, God will empower us to do great things. Continue to seek God through these avenues, and you will receive revelation that will help you in your life. One might read the previous chapters and surmise that prayer is like waving a magic wand; and with just one wave, brokenness will be mended. This cannot be further from the truth; prayer is not always a quick fix. God does not answer our prayer in our timeframe, but we must continually seek God.

CHAPTER 4
POWERING ON

"Pray without ceasing" (1 Thessalonians 5:17).

HITTING THE POWER BUTTON

The power button must be pushed for the machine to operate. Pressing the power button gives life to the device. Normally, a green, orange or yellow light will light up, which tells the user that the device is on, allowing the user to see the screen displaying the programs on the device.

POWERING ON PRAYER

When it comes to prayer, powering on is the process of beginning a prayer. It is the moment when one starts praying. "Dear God" is a common way that people start prayer; or another way is saying, "Gracious, Heavenly Father." In both instances, the individual recognizes God by title.

Look at how King David began his prayer. Psalm 25:1 records: "In you, LORD my God, I put my trust." With these fine words, David recognizes that God is the One in Whom he places his trust. His spiritual antenna was up and cognizant of the fact that God is reliable.

We learn from David that we may begin our prayer with a description of God's character. For example, in Psalm 25, David testifies that God is trustworthy. Our prayers may be around the trustworthiness of God. We may recount ways that God has been trustworthy in our lives.

ENTERING GOD'S PRESENCE

After powering on a mobile device, a passcode may be entered to access the programs on a computer. Usually, these are codes that have some type of significance to someone. This ensures device security.

Similar to one entering a passcode to have access to a computer, iPad, or smartphone, petitions are our entry to God's presence. One enters their likes, dislikes, and areas of interest in the form of a petition to God with the goal of the Lord doing something about the situation. Overall, these petitions convey what we are feeling about a certain matter. "Lord, I am feeling overwhelming anxiety about my first day of work." "I am feeling angry about something that I witnessed." These are ways that we begin a prayer.

DELIVERANCE

Entering God's presence opens the door for our deliverance. Deliverance means being set free. Scripture provides countless examples of deliverance. The Prophet Elijah received the deliverance from a challenging situation.

Entering God's presence also helped Elijah walk in his deliverance from depression. Literally, he walked out of the cave and into his God-appointed purpose (1 Kings 19:15). Verse fifteen says, "The LORD said to him, 'Go back the way you came, and go to the Desert of Damascus. When you get there, anoint HAZAEL king over Aram." God called him out of his rut in order to minister to other people. He was able to move forward in life. It appears that his prayer was beneficial. In the end, Elijah developed a deeper level of trust in the Lord because of his ordeal. His dependence on the Lord grew from this incident. His eyes appeared to be open to the fact that God exceeded expectations.

In my life, God delivered me from road rage. Cars traveling too close to me irritated me. Drivers who don't use signals would strike a chord as well. I would allow other people to anger me to the point of causing me to boil. As

I prepared to exit a highway in June of 2018, there was a car on the shoulder that started to cut in front of my vehicle. The driver and I made eye contact. He had a confused look on his face by the fact that I didn't yield the right of way to him. I mocked him and continued driving. As I was down the ramp, he and I made eye contact again. This time, he and his passenger pointed their middle fingers up at me. A surge of anger flowed through my body and I blew the horn for a long time. Even thoughts of confronting the drivers went through my mind.

Following this occurrence, I was still angry for almost an hour. I spoke to my wife, and she admonished me for my behavior. She highlighted the fact that I needed to let things go and not get so worked up. At this point, I realized that I have road rage that needed to be delivered from this immense anger. The only way this issue would be handled is by praying to God.

On that day, I prayed and asked for deliverance from my anger. Part of my petition was that God would take control of my emotions so that other people's behavior wouldn't put a damper on my spirit. Some of the strategies that the Lord has imparted upon me and continues to help me with is not looking at some of the other drivers in the road and not staring out of my rearview mirror at drivers who drive too close. These strategies help me to focus on my driving and not the cars around me.

What I learned from this event and is not to allow other drivers have power over me. In other terms, I need to stop allowing the poor decisions of other drivers to rouse me up. I am glad to report that this ongoing prayer continues to deliver me from road rage. I don't get nearly as upset when drivers do things that rub me the wrong way. I don't give as much attention as in the past to ignorant drivers. These strategies give me relief.

God uses prayer to allow us to walk in our deliverance. We can move past negative emotions with the help of God. We can walk away from the quicksand that attempts to get us stuck in life. It's time for us to walk in this liberation and release.

Entering the presence of the Lord will make a difference in your life. You will experience a sharper focus and deliverance. A sharper focus helps you align with the purpose that God has for you. The deliverance may come in the form of realizing that a negative circumstance doesn't have control over you.

SHARPER FOCUS

A sharper focus is a fruit of deliverance. We learn from Elijah's situation that we will have a sharper focus in life. He mentored Elisha, another great prophet of Israel (1 Kings 19:21). He put time, energy, and attention in ensuring that Elisha developed the skills that he needed to become a prophet who would teach the people of Israel the way of the Lord. What enabled Elijah to fulfill this ministerial responsibility was his sharp focus on the Lord.

A sharper focus is time spent with the Lord. It takes my mind off other things. At times, what I find is that the Lord occupies my thoughts and feelings during prayer. I can pay attention to the things that God wants me to pay attention to. This may include preparing for sermons or creating Bible studies. Prayer becomes invaluable time.

ILLUSTRATION

Over the past two years, my church has experienced multiple deaths. The people we lost were pillars of the church and their communities. Deeply saddened by these losses, I felt led by the Spirit of God to have a prayer and healing service. This service would give the church the opportunity to grieve and cry out to the Lord with our overwhelming emotions. In a time of sharing, we were able to acknowledge our pain. We did this by having a moment of silence to remember the lives that had been lost. Members seemed to be cultivated to God as our healing begun.

The church developed a sharper focus on the Lord by fulfilling God's purpose. We continue to strive to be a praying church and having an additional prayer service that helps us meet our purpose. Additionally, we realized that we needed to acknowledge our hurt to begin to experience our healing. We couldn't ignore our pain and expect to feel the presence of God within our hearts.

In closing, prayer in Jesus' name is like entering a code and having access to the heart of God because of the unique closeness of the relationship between Christ and God. Using these three words indicates that we pray in agreement with the will and plan of God.

CHAPTER 5
THE MOST RELIABLE WIRELESS COMMUNICATION

"Call to me and I will answer you and tell you great and unsearchable things you do not know" (Jeremiah 33:3).

The most reliable wireless communication is not smartphones, iPads, or laptops, but prayer.

With an unlimited global connection and no restricted coverage areas,

It easily covers the largest network—humanity, the planet, fish, and birds.

As for late fees or hidden charges, they do not exist.

There is no cost, but time and devotion to Jesus.

And it's amazing that the Lord is always on the other end of our call.

Isn't that a blessing?

When looking at wireless communication, remember prayer is the best option.

Every wireless provider highlights what sets it apart from the rest. Often, it's internet speed, data storage, and the cost of the service. The truth is that prayer stands out from all other wireless communication. With that said, I will extract four points that I think demonstrate the superiority of prayer over other forms of wireless communication.

REASON #1: ALWAYS CONNECTED

"You have searched me, LORD, and you know me. You know when I sit and when I rise; you perceive my thoughts from afar" (Psalm 139:1-2).

Just the other day, I was on the phone with a Verizon customer service representative and inquired about a new phone because of issues that I had with my phone. After briefly speaking with the representative, I lost my connection, and the phone call dropped. Unfortunately, this happened multiple times. As I waited to connect with the service provider, it was confirmed in my mind that I needed a reliable cell phone. During this time, I couldn't get my questions answered because of the disruption. This put me and my communication in limbo.

DISRUPTIONS IN COVERAGE

When trying to secure a solid internet connection, one must also be concerned about Network Wireless Interference. Network Wireless Interference is a barrier to wireless communication. Network interference is when "signals operating at similar frequencies get crossed which causes interference which has a significantly negative effect on the performance of the network." If there are too many wireless signals within an area, one may have difficulties connecting to the internet.

Additionally, trees, power outages, and buildings may stand in the way of wireless communication. As a result of these hindrances, slow, unstable and insecure wireless network may occur. Many things may interfere with a wireless network: everything from the Wi-Fi networks of neighbors, old firmware, humans."[9] This means that objects and even networks can halt wireless service.

---

[9] Jeff Bertolucci, "Six Things That Block Your WiFi, and How to Fix Them" https://www.pcworld.com/article/227973/six_things_that_block_your_wifi_and_how_to_fix_them.html?page=2 (accessed May 29, 2019).

Natural events and disasters may also disrupt service. Severe thunderstorms may cause the power to go out, disrupting internet service. Hurricanes and catastrophic flooding may obstruct the use of wireless devices because there is no signal. Not to mention that mobile devices need to be charged for them to be used. Unfortunately, one may use his or her device during the storm only until the battery dies on the mobile device. After the battery dies, one will not be able to use the device until electricity is restored. Never has this been more apparent than with Hurricane Harvey. Epic rain and flooding annihilated homes, roads, and communities. During this disaster, many people lost their power, which meant they could not use their wireless devices and couldn't communicate with others.

Additionally, when one flies on an airplane, mobile users must turn their mobile devices off or place them in airplane mode. Airplane mode means that the passenger cannot receive calls, connect to the internet, or send text messages unless one uses their own Wi-Fi, which is not always reliable. If plane passengers use their mobile devices, they can produce radio signals that can obstruct with communications within the aircraft communications. This confusion means that the communication may be skewed and unreliable. In the end, passengers cannot communicate with those who are not on the plane.

THE RELIABLE CONNECTION

Wouldn't it be nice to have wireless communication that stays connected regardless of the environment? Wouldn't it be nice to have wireless communication that stays connected even if there are power outages? Wouldn't it be nice if there was a form of wireless communication that always stayed connected no matter the altitude? Wouldn't it be nice to always have wireless communication no matter the weather conditions? The good news is that you can.

Prayer is the only form of wireless communication that none of these physical impediments can disrupt. Absolutely nothing can get in the way of us turning to God in prayer. This is great news!

Prayer provides us with an impeccable and efficient method of wireless communication which our current wireless devices cannot provide. Prayer provides us with around-the-clock coverage because "God never sleeps nor slumbers" (Psalm 121:4). This Scripture suggests that God is always attentive. Furthermore, when the electricity is out, prayer still works. When the atmosphere suddenly becomes unsafe, prayer still works because God is paying attention to human conditions and circumstances.

I prayed during some of the worst storms and felt an overwhelming calmness. I sensed God's loving arms wrapping around me and keeping me safe. In other terms, I have experienced the peace and serenity of the presence of God.

Jesus heartens His disciples to stay connected to God in an account in Matthew 26:40. Prior to Jesus' death, He went to the Garden of Gethsemane to pray. After praying for a long period of time, He returned to His disciples and found them asleep. He admonished His disciples to stay awake and pray to the Lord. He used the words, "Couldn't you men keep watch with me for one hour?" Within this story, they continued to fall asleep when they were commanded by Jesus to pray. The meaning behind Jesus' words is that the disciples needed to keep in communication with God and not allow their feelings of fatigue to stop them from praying.

Like the disciples, we need to stay awake and connected to God. We need to constantly pray to do God's will. This may mean fighting fatigue to talk with God. This may mean fighting through some pain to get to God. This may mean turning the television off so that we may pray to God.

We need to take advantage of this always-open prayer line that we have with God. During different times of our day, we need to devote time in prayer. We can take those opportunities to seek the Lord. My personal advice is to start the day with prayer. We never know the challenges that the day will bring. We never know if we will get through the day, so, it is better to start the day with prayer.

Through prayer, we are always connected to God. We are always able to pray anytime day or night. Above, I mentioned prayer from the standpoint that prayer is always open, but the question is, are we always willing to pray? Are we willing to talk to the Most High? Are we willing to push ourselves to pray? These are the questions that we must ask ourselves if we truly want to be connected to God. I strongly encourage everyone to pray. Take advantage of silent opportunities to connect with the Creator. When on a flight, on a long drive, or maybe on a cruise, please seek the Lord. The results will bless and strengthen you and others because prayer is time well spent.

REASON #2: THE SECURE LINE

"You discern my going out and my lying down; you are familiar with all my ways" (Psalm 139:3).

Unfortunately, the downside to wireless networks is that they are not always secure. This means that hackers may have access to your web browsing history, and there is a potential risk when you bank online because dishonest people can have access to your account information and steal your money and identity.

The reasons mentioned accentuate why network security is essential to mobile users. Consumers want to ensure that their confidential information remains private. This may include documents and pictures, among other things. Therefore, device passcodes to protect data are strongly encouraged by many network providers.

In recent years in the United States, cyber security is a major issue. Just look at the first day of the Democratic National Convention in 2016 when former Secretary of State Hillary Clinton's emails appeared to be hacked.

Contents of her emails were made available to the public. This is problematic because confidential information is not concealed and protected and can get into the hands of people with ill intentions.

There are some serious concerns about the 2020 United States Presidential election that a foreign government could interfere in the election.[10] Apprehension about misinformation campaigns intended to smear and spread false information about one candidate is possible during this time of cyber insecurity. This may create doubt and uncertainty among voters and discourage them from showing up to the polls. These are examples of insecure forms of wireless communication.

THE SECURITY OF PRAYER

Unlike the occasional security breaches with wireless networks, prayer is always secure. We never have to worry about invasions of privacy. We don't have to worry about people hacking our prayers. We can tell God what is on our minds and not be concerned about being overheard by others; so, we feel safe. The next paragraph gives us a biblical example.

There is evidence in the Sacred Scriptures that suggests Jesus' secure connection to God was on display at His death on Calvary in Luke 23. Even during Jesus' impending death, He was not deterred from praying. While hanging on the cross, Jesus prayed for those who were persecuting Him. In the Gospel of Luke, the author records Jesus saying these words: "Father, forgive them, for they do not know what they are doing" (Luke 23:34). Talk about no barrier between humanity and God. This means that death, struggle, and hardship did not keep Jesus from praying to God.

In summary, prayer is the secure source of wireless communication. We can speak our mind to God and not have to worry about third-party

---

10 Erin Banco, "FBI Director Christopher Wray Says Russia Remains a Threat to 2020 Election," TheDailyBeast.com, https://www.thedailybeast.com/fbi-director-christopher-wray-says-russia-remains-a-threat-to-2020-election (accessed April 27, 2019).

interference. We do not have to worry about our information being made public when we talk to the Lord. The same cannot be said about our mobile wireless devices in this age of security breaches and cyber corruption. Yet, prayer affords us a safe way to contact, communicate, and commune with the living God and not worry about distractions. In the end, we will experience peace and focus as we move forward in our endeavors. If you want a secure source of wireless communication, try prayer.

REASON #3: RELIABLE GLOBAL COVERAGE

"For the LORD your God goes with you; he will never leave you nor forsake you" (Deuteroonomy 31:6).

Regrettably, mobile technology does not always provide dependable global coverage. Have you ever noticed that it is difficult to access friends and family via a smartphone while overseas? Some smartphones do not work overseas. This means that smartphone communication may not be a viable option for international communication.

Another issue that consumers face when they travel out of the country is the roaming and international charges on phone calls. Some people cannot afford these costs and don't communicate on trips via their cell phones. Based on a CNN money report in 2015, "Verizon charges $10 a day for roaming and international charges."[11] What a hassle! So, if I go to a foreign country, this will be seventy dollars on top of hotel costs, food costs, and other costs, which is far too expensive for some. Yet, there is a free option that is a far more reliable mode of wireless communication that has no geographic restrictions.

Unlike mobile devices, which are not always reliable sources of communication in foreign areas, Jesus offers free global range of communication in

---

11 Hope King, "Verizon Now Charges $10 a Day for International Roaming," CNN.com, www.money.cnn.com/2015/11/12/technology/verizon-travelpass/ (accessed September 10, 2017).

prayer. John 17:20 foreshadows Jesus praying for people locally, abroad, and even in the future. Read these touching words: "My prayer is not for them alone. I pray also for those who will believe in me through their message." In verse twenty-one, Jesus prays for different countries and continents: "That all of them may be one, Father, just as you are in me and I am in you. May they also be in us so that the world may believe that you have sent me."

Prayer even offers reliable global coverage. Tell me what other device beats that! Prayer connects people instantly to God. Every year for the past twenty-four years, Unity Village—a worldwide movement of an interfaith community—hosts a yearly World Day of Prayer. Friday, September 14, 2017, was Unity World Day of Prayer, which took place in Unity Village in Minneapolis, Minnesota. The day has a prayer emphasis on unity, meditation, peace, and the oneness of humanity with God. This dynamic event includes meditation, prayer vigils, prayer requests, and prayerful readings. During this day, people from around the world pray for others from different countries to be unified in thought and harmony. According to Rev. Linda Martella-Whitsett, Unity Minister and speaker, prayer equals "spiritual strength to navigate the time and space that we occupy."[12] Additionally, this means that we have the fortitude to move through the enjoyable, perplexing, and disappointing times in life.

RELIABLE GLOBAL COVERAGE IN THE BIBLE

Geographically, a reliable global coverage plays out in Jesus' earthly ministry by way of prayer. We see Jesus praying in Jerusalem, Bethany, and Calvary throughout his ministry. In Matthew 26:36-46, Jesus prayed in the Garden of Gethsemane to prepare for His death, which means that prayer worked in a deserted garden area. In Luke 18:10, two men went to the temple to pray. This shows us that prayer works in a spiritual atmosphere. In John 11:38-44, Jesus

---

[12] Rev. Linda-Martella Whitsett, https://www.youtube.com/watch?v=DM8fw2nb7ek (accessed on September 27, 2017).

restores Lazarus to life in Bethany through prayer, which demonstrates that prayer also works in a home environment.

Just in case you wondered whether the Gospel accounts are the only examples of global coverage of prayer, the answer is no. Paul prayed even from prison (Acts 16). Elijah prayed even in seclusion and isolation in a cave far from any recognized place of worship (1 Kings 19). Moses prayed on Mount Sinai (Exodus 32:9-14). These examples tell us that God is always available to us through prayer, regardless of our geographic location.

The reliable global coverage that prayer offers is a necessity because of its widespread impact. As mentioned, it influences people from all over the world. Consequently, prayer has the power to touch people in different places, which speak to its unlimited reach. Ultimately, this is dependable communication.

REASON# 4: THE PERFECT ROUTER

"Before a word is on my tongue you, Lord, know it completely" (Psalm 139:4).

Routers are small electronic devices that bring multiple computer networks together through either wired or wireless connections. A router needs Wi-Fi to connect to the internet in residential and commercial areas. You would think that this works seamlessly. Yet, there are many problems with routers, such as slow data speeds and dead spots.

Slow data speeds mean that the internet will move at a snail's pace, which may take minutes to access a website. In other cases, slow data speeds may time out internet searches. In both instances, the internet doesn't work as it should because usually one is able to access the internet within seconds.

Dead spots are also troublesome because one is unable to get service. One may walk into a room where there is a dead zone, and communication will abruptly stop. At work, I have a dead zone area in my cubicle, and my signal gets lost. Wouldn't it be nice to have wireless communication without dead spots and wireless dead zones?

ROUTING OUR REQUESTS TO GOD

Dissimilar from wireless routers that sometimes have malfunctions, prayer is the perfect router. It will always forward data (our requests) to the network (God), so there is a strong Earth-to-Heaven and Heaven-to-Earth connection. There is no slow data speed or dead spots with prayer. In fact, prayer routes our concerns, burdens, and requests upward to God. The Scripture says, "Cast your cares on the LORD and he will sustain you" (Psalm 55:22). This means laying down our problems, which will bring relief in our lives.

King David routes what weighs heavily on his heart to God in Psalm 109. To provide some context for the psalm, David is immensely troubled by his adversaries. In fact, he conveys that he is unjustly attacked (v. 3). However, he chooses to make a plea before God in verse twenty-six: "Help me, LORD my God; save me according to your unfailing love." David asks for the Lord's help in governing the matters of life.

With prayer, we will release our problems to the Lord. Let the following words from Psalm 55:22 marinate on your mind and heart: "Pile your troubles on God's shoulders—he'll carry your load; he'll help you out. He'll never let good people topple into ruin (MSG)." Another way of saying this is that prayer allows us to transfer data to God in the form of thanksgiving, confession, supplication, and adoration to the Lord; and He will handle everything.

Releasing our problems to the Lord is what will greatly help North America and the U.K. in this contentious political season. There is a lot of tension in North America and in the U.K. around social issues of immigration, health care, gun control, tax reform, and race relations, which causes anxiety and unrest. As a result, government officials are at odds on how to address these complex issues, which cause disunity and divisiveness. Yet in times like these, we need to turn to God because we do not know what the future holds, but we know who holds the future. Proverbs 16:1 phrases my point this way: "Mortals make elaborate plans, but GOD has the last word" (The Message). Look at God like the train conductor who operates the train, making sure that the ride is smooth and that the train gets to its destination. We must realize that power doesn't lie with any human, but with the Divine. Now, I will provide examples of biblically based routed prayers in the form of adoration, confession, thanksgiving, and supplication, also known as ACTS.

UPWARD MOBILITY

Routing our prayers to God is a sign of upward mobility. We take our request upward to God. Acts 9 presents the salvation story of Paul during the Road to Damascus. Paul's supernatural experience with God can be described as the upward movement in prayer. We envision Paul looking up to the Lord with a spirit of humility and receiving Divine-human intimacy. The upward motion of prayer builds and sustains our relationship with God with intimacy through love. We can seek, find, establish, and reestablish our connection with the Lord.

EXAMPLE

An image that popped into my mind about upward mobility is the story of a young female that was a victim of the horrific storm Hurricane Harvey that hit Texas in 2017. In an interview she said that she looked up and waited for the helicopter to come and rescue her and her family. The woman's home was flooded, and the only method of escape would have to come from above. Eventually, a helicopter saw her and came to her rescue. The helicopter saved her and her family from a dangerous situation.

We, too, must look up for help. We will learn in life that looking to the right and to the left will be of no benefit, and the only way that we will have our needs met is by looking up to God. The psalm writer is correct in asserting, "I lift up my eyes to the mountains—where does my help come from? My help comes from the Lord, the Maker of heaven and earth" (Psalm 121:1-2, NIV). We must continue to look up and call for help.

Upward mobility is the groundwork for intimacy with God. Intimacy with God moves us beyond practicing prayer simply as a learned behavior. We desire to pray because we love God. It involves making some quiet time so that we can be attentive to God. It heightens our senses and enables us to center ourselves on God. This intimate time in prayer with God is like taking the essential vitamins and minerals needed for the body to operate and function properly.

Throughout Jesus' temporary, but productive, three-year, itinerant, earthly ministry, He spent an exceptional amount of time in prayer. While His disciples were falling asleep and engaged in other things, we find Jesus absorbed in prayer (Matt. 26:40). From Jesus, we learn that prayer prepares us for what life brings as we have a calming Force Who will help, prepare, equip, and instruct us through the demands in life.

In the Holy Writ, Jesus portrays upward mobility in His prayer time by sharing His innermost feelings with God. Mark 1:35 tells us that Jesus rose early in the morning and prayed. The magnitude of the prayer increased as He continued to preach the Gospel and drive out demons (Mark 1:39).

Through God, prayer helps us to orient ourselves to the purpose and plans that God has for our lives. Think about the individual who wakes up but is not ready to get out of the bed because his or her body is not oriented or ready to begin the new day. Perhaps one's eyes are open, but the body isn't ready to move. This illustration intends to make the point that prayer not only opens our eyes, but also allows our body to align with the plans of God for our lives.

The purpose of the prayer is for the follower to develop an intimate relationship with the Divine which demonstrates his or her love for God. It is not enough to make our requests known before God. We must pray following God's rules, aligned with God's will for the purpose of communicating with the Creator. This means that prayer is the tool that helps keep us in our search for the Lord.

I encourage you to send a "tweet" (message) to God through prayer. Let God know what is on your mind. Share with God the anxieties, stressors, and joys of your life. Acknowledge that the Lord is the One Who provided you with traveling mercies to your destinations of the day. Admit that God is the One Who provides food on your table and clothes on your back. Declare that God is the One Who will help you, even when everyone else turns their back on you. Use this spiritual "Twitter" function through prayer.

Well, prayer can be looked at as one speaking a text message to God. It can go something like this: "Good morning, Lord. Thanks for giving me a new day of life. Thank You for giving me a right mind today." Just saying these words can brighten up one's day.

ADORATION

We route our prayers of adoration to God. Adoration is worshiping the true God. Revelation 4:11 demonstrates a prayer of adoration: "You are worthy, our Lord and God, to receive glory and honor and power, for you created all things, and by your will they were created and have their being." Here the author of Revelation declares admiration for the living God. Adoring God means acknowledging the magnificence of creation is beautiful and appealing.

Think about how strangers adore a baby or small child. They find these young individuals precious and may smile and wave at them. These individuals are drawn to the babies and little people because of their innocence and because they consider them cute.

On a much larger scale, we adore the fact that God is precious. God is the Source of everything, which makes God adorable. This means to hold God in the highest esteem.

CONFESSION

We can route our prayers of confession to God. A prayer of confession is an expression of contrition to God. Psalm 51:1-2 shows us a prayer of confession from the lips of King David. "Have mercy on me, O God, according to your unfailing love; according to your great compassion blot out my transgressions. Wash away all my iniquity and cleanse me from my sin." David expresses his contrition before the Lord for committing adultery with Bathsheba. He wanted pardon for his mistake.

A prayer of confession is also an approach to get things off your chest. We can admit and acknowledge our wrongdoing. We can vocalize these things, which will, in turn, give us a clear head.

Confession is like bench pressing the weight of our mistakes to God. We no longer must hold the weight of our failures and mistakes but, through prayer, are able to turn our mistakes upward to God. The key is that God hears our sincere confession.

Finally, confession is the initial step toward deliverance. We are delivered from self-pity and regret and can be in a space where we are able to receive the joy that the Lord gives. One must acknowledge their shortcomings, or mistake before one is able to move forward.

THANKSGIVING

We can route our prayers of thanksgiving or gratitude to the Lord. Psalm 111:1-5 has this type of an exemplary prayer:

> Praise the Lord. I will extol the Lord with all my heart in the council of the upright and in the assembly. Great are the works of

the Lord; they are pondered by all who delight in them. Glorious and majestic are his deeds, and his righteousness endures forever. He has caused his wonders to be remembered; the Lord is gracious and compassionate. He provides food for those who fear him; he remembers his covenant forever.

Notice that this prayer of thanksgiving completely focuses on God. It focuses on the character of God ("majestic are His deeds"). Prayers of thanksgiving are ways to pray and not be self-centered.

A contemporary way of expressing our thankfulness to God may be to thank the Lord for waking us up this day and clothing us in our right mind. Thank God for the activity of our limbs and for the opportunity to pray.

SUPPLICATION

We can route our supplications or needs to the Lord. This may be for a clear mind and physical strength. Second Chronicles 6:19 says, "Yet, Lord my God, give attention to your servant's prayer and his plea for mercy. Hear the cry and the prayer that your servant is praying in your presence." Here he is praying for God's attention, which seems to be an immediate need.

There are varying needs that humans have. These may include physical, emotional, financial, etc. The good thing is that we can route our specific needs to the One who can address them.

Today, this takes place when we admit to God what is going on with us. We bring the request to God with the foreknowledge that God will listen and address our situation the way that God sees fit. We give that situation to God and wait to see what direction God will take in handling the situation.

A point of clarification to my earlier point is that we continue to pursue God in supplication. It is not a one-time prayer event. Constant and consistent prayer is needed.

Recently, I had a prayer of supplication that came up. A couple of months ago, I asked the Lord for some guidance to deal with a situation that came up on my job. I made a speech to a group of people, and an individual was offended by a gesture that I made. She sent me a long text message about how my gesture rubbed her the wrong way. I had no intention of offending this individual but realized that I needed to address her. After praying about the situation, I got some advice from two Christians to whom I am close. I took their advice and rectified the situation.

What worked in my situation is that I made my concern known to my friends and allowed them to guide me through the ordeal. I didn't put my two cents in the situation, which would have defeated the purpose of me calling to get their advice.

A prayer of supplication is like the experience that I went through when I sought guidance from my friends. I had to communicate my issue and allow them to direct me to the proper way to handle the situation.

Prayer is the perfect router because it takes our requests of adoration, confession, thanksgiving, and supplication to God. When our requests get to the right Source, breakthroughs and restoration may take place. Not having to deal with slow data speeds and dead zone areas make prayer that much more appealing. Please pray because it will ignite change in your life.

CHAPTER 6

7 KEYS TO EXPERIENCING GOD'S PRESENCE AND POWER

"I will give you the keys of the kingdom of heaven" (Matthew 16:19).

Experiencing God's presence and power are important because we can grow in our relationship through our encounters with God through prayer. When we spend time with God, we are usually able to become aware of other qualities of God. For instance, there have been times that I have offered God praise for God's blessings of health and financial stability, and God revealed to me how He also protected me from harm. This means that not only did I view God as a Provider, but also as a Protector.

Another way that we may understand the significance of the experience of God is through the analogy of fans going to a concert. Fans go to a concert to hear music for the energy and the excitement that the artist brings. Usually, fans become wrapped in the moment at concerts and will start singing and even dancing with the artist. This experience is only possible by attending a concert.

In a similar way, prayer is a unique, spiritual experience when we can talk to our Creator. We can feel God in our space, hearts, and dwelling, and prayer brings an excitement and eagerness to be in the presence of the Lord. Below are seven keys to depict crucial aspects that we should incorporate into our prayer lives.

KEY # 1: INTROSPECTION

"Examine yourselves to see whether you are in the faith" (2 Corinthians 13:5).

Has a problem ever weighed heavily on your mind to the point that you sat in silence trying to come up with the solution? This process is called **introspection**, the number one key of prayer, and it reflects the inward motion of prayer.

INWARD MOVEMENT

Introspection and prayer intersect. According to an online dictionary reference, *introspection* is defined as "observation or examination of one's own mental and emotional state, mental processes, etc.; the act of looking within oneself."[13] Based on the definition, much of introspection focuses on our thought process, which is how we arrive at decisions. For instance, secretly praying for others to fail in their pursuit of achieving goals makes known our character flaws. It is important to note that introspection should take place prior to and during our prayer time.

Introspection reveals our character, and prayer demonstrates our priorities. Prayer shows what matters the most to us and how we devote our time. Praying a lot for ways to help the hungry to be fed demonstrates that the poor are important to the one praying. As proclaimed by Buddhist teacher Jan Chozen Bays, "Prayer is an inward turn of our hearts and minds toward the positive qualities of compassion and clarity."[14] These qualities convey the significance of our interactions with others as opposed to the things that we can gain. With this type of prayer, other people are the priority, instead of the prosperity of the one praying. At its core, we gain a better understanding of self through introspection and prayer.

---

[13] *Dictionary.com*, s.v. "introspection," www.dictionary.com (accessed December 6, 2018).
[14] Sam Littlefair, "Do Buddhists Pray? What For?," Lions Roar.com, www.lionsroar.com what-is-prayer-in-buddhism/ (accessed August 16, 2017).

BIBLICAL EXAMPLE

Introspection is discussed in the New Testament about the Eucharist (The Lord's Supper also known as communion). I Corinthians 11:28 records that "everyone ought to examine themselves before they eat of the bread and drink from the cup." This self-reflection allows one to confess any sins to the Lord before eating the Holy Meal. During this pre-communion time, the congregant analyzes his or herself and actions and determines whether he or she is holding any grudges or bitterness toward his or her neighbor. Based on this self-examination, a person comes to the decision of whether he or she should or should not come to partake of the Holy Communion because of unforgiveness or for holding a grudge against another individual.

EXAMPLE

Currently, I am going through the elder ordination process of the United Methodist Church and have frequently conducted a self-analysis of my motives to become ordained. In the silence, I ask myself several questions: What is my motivation for wanting to become an ordained minister within the United Methodist Church? Am I power hungry? Do I want name recognition? Do I want an increase in salary? What is the real reason that I want to become ordained? Am I okay with being reassigned to a new church every few years? These are introspective questions that allow me to get to my true motives.

Therefore, personal examination includes a thorough evaluation of thoughts, emotions, and actions. And we can only do this when we are sitting in silence in prayer. In Lamentations 3:40, the prophet Jeremiah encapsulates this point by penning these thought-provoking words: "Let us examine our ways and test them and let us return to the LORD." He wrote this to hearten the Israelites to chase God and not worthless idols after they endured the destruction of Jerusalem.

Another way of looking at introspection is viewing it as a time of gathering our thoughts. In other words, Jeremiah wanted the Israelites to shut themselves out from idols (Jeremiah 10), so they would be alone with God during worship. In Luke 5:16, Jesus is alone in the Garden of Gethsemane, gathering His thoughts and emotions prior to His brutal crucifixion that would shortly follow. With the Israelites and Jesus, both needed that quiet space to look to the Lord without the competing voices or activities that vie for their time and attention.

Distancing ourselves from the distractions of life is the key to introspection. Silencing cell phones and turning off our computers are ways that we can focus on the Lord in introspection prior to prayer. Tuning out these distractions allows us to tune into God.

Introspection also exposes sin and the unpleasant things in our lives. The Lord wants us to examine ourselves to determine whether we have any sin within us. Galatians 6:4-5 says, "Each one should test their own actions. Then they can take pride in themselves alone, without comparing themselves to someone else, for each one should carry their own load." Sometimes, while we sit in silence, we can identify personal sin. During this reflection, we deduce that we should confess our sins. Therefore, "we confess our sins, [God] is faithful and just and will forgive us our sins and purify us from all unrighteousness" (1 John 1:9). Introspection leads us to confession, which leads to entering a relationship with God. Our times of introspection will line us up with the Word of God. Scripture must govern our self-evaluation. In other words, when we reflect on different matters, we must do so according to the Holy Word.

Introspection should be a common practice in your day-to-day decisions. You always want to make sure that you are making the right decisions for the right reasons. The right reason is one that is aligned with the Word and will of God, and introspection helps to reveal God's will. In the morning, before starting the day, take a moment and have a silent reflection. In this reflection, look and analyze your motives and how to approach the tasks for the day. What happens in introspection is that the Lord gives clarity on matters. You can move forward in life knowing full well that you are doing things the way that God desired.

For instance, in times of introspection, you may receive guidance about how to approach relational issues with others. Introspection gives you the time and space and clarity of thought to hear and receive a Word from the Lord, which is a time of revelation. Your innermost feelings and emotions surface in times of introspection. I can't state the many times that I received clarity about how to handle situations through silent times of reflection.

Introspection is crucial because we better understand what we need to pray about. We better understand our needs and areas that we need to grow. This time of introspection sets the stage for our time of prayer.

KEY #2: DRIVEN BY FAITH

"When you pass through the waters, I will be with you" (Isaiah 43:2).

Driving requires fuel to get the car from point A to point B. Fuel is the power that enables the car to run. In addition, one needs to put their hands on the steering wheel and his or her foot on the gas for the vehicle to drive.

In a similar manner, faith is the fuel that drives our prayers. Faith provides the power needed to move the hands of God to intervene in a situation. Faith is what puts us in right standing with God. This means "to act justly, and to love mercy, and to walk humbly with our God" (Micah 6:8). Right standing with God is the same as being in one accord with the living God. Below, I discuss faith in more detail.

ROOTED IN FAITH

The second key to having an effective prayer life is that our prayers should be **rooted in faith.** Faith is the legs that enable a prayer to stand and reach God. Here is what the letter to the Hebrews tells us about faith: "Now faith is confidence in what we hope for and assurance about what we do not see" (Hebrews 11:1). In a nutshell, this passage addresses the fact that faith is what brings hope to life.

Our prayers need to be grounded in our steady conviction that God is present in our situations or ordeals. For example, in the above text, James provides his audience with a fundamental lesson on faith. He tells them that faith goes hand in hand with prayer, letting them know that the faith behind the prayer is what causes things to happen.

A LITTLE BIT OF FAITH GOES A LONG WAY

Sometimes, when using a mobile device, one does not need great signal strength to be able to communicate. For instance, there have been times when I was in a dead zone but had a signal long enough to be able to make a quick call and communicate what I needed to communicate before the call was terminated. These conversations have been short, but productive, conversations.

This cellular signal is like our faith; Jesus teaches us that it only takes a little faith to do great things. The Scripture states that "faith as small as a mustard seed" removes mountains (Matthew 17:20 and Luke 17:6). A little bit of faith will go a long way in our lives. We must utilize our faith which will assist us in our lives.

Faith is what helps us get through the valleys in life. Faith is what gets us through sickness, pain, and other difficulties. Faith is the engine that drives our prayers and allows the human-to-Divine connection to occur. James 5:15 says, "The prayer offered in faith will make the sick person well." This suggests that faith is the device used to bring about healing.

BIBLICAL EXAMPLES OF FAITH

Within James 5:17-18, James points to the prophet Elijah as someone who walked by faith. In verse seventeen, Elijah prayed that it would stop raining;

God granted his request. In fact, for three-and-a-half years, it didn't rain. In verse eighteen, Elijah prayed for it to start raining, and it rained. It appears that God responded to Elijah's petition because of Elijah's faith.

Another example of a prayer of faith is Jesus' healing of Lazarus. In John 11:38-44, John reveals in this moving account that the prayer of faith is what raised Lazarus from the dead. "So they took away the stone. Then Jesus looked up and said, 'Father, I thank you that you have heard me. I knew that you always hear me, but I said this for the benefit of the people standing here, that they may believe that you sent me'" (vs. 41-42). In other words, Jesus spoke confidentially to God and wanted God to perform this miracle so people would know that He is the Son of God. Clearly, the words of Jesus were emblematic of His faith. He spoke with authority and confidence, knowing that Lazarus would be revived. In the end, Lazarus gets up. "The dead man came out, his hands and feet wrapped with strips of linen, and a cloth around his face" (v. 44). The take-away point is that faith manifests itself in confidence, which leads to change.

When we pray, we must believe that our prayer will come to fruition. Eleven years ago, a loved one had heart surgery and was hospitalized. This was a very emotionally intense time for my family. I visited my loved one and would pray for him. During those prayers, doubt and fear would attempt to creep in to dissuade me from thinking that my loved one would be healed. I remember rebuking those thoughts, feelings, and emotions and believing in their healing. A few weeks later, the doctors stated that his heart was healthy. Following the surgery, my loved one lost weight. I strongly believe that my faith that my relative would be healed is what helped him. God was able to hear and answer my prayers due to my faith. God receives the prayer of faith (James 5:15).

Concretely, faith anticipates with hopeful expectation what the senses cannot. Here are some examples of some faith statements: "By faith, I expect to receive supernatural healing from my sickness." "By faith, I expect to make the honor roll this semester." "By faith, I expect for my broken relationships to become whole." Faith goes beyond the prevailing evidence in our situations.

Sometimes, we will pray and will not get our desired results. Guess what we should do in these situations? We need to keep praying and not lose hope. God may have another plan in store for us. First Thessalonians 5:17 tells us to "pray continually."

By no means am I making the contention that the only people who pray are people of faith. That is simply untrue and not the point that I am making. However, the overarching point behind this chapter is that we should allow our doubts and insecurities to lead us to pray. Allow those things that bother us to direct us to a place of prayer.

Our prayers need to be driven by faith. Faith is the foundation to a productive prayer life. Believe in faith that whatever you pray for will come to fruition in the way that God has planned. Remember that faith is the medium that helps our prayers reach God's ears. We must approach God in faith.

KEY #3: A SINCERE HEART

"Let us draw near to God with a sincere heart and with the full assurance that faith brings" (Hebrews 10:22).

The window of God's heart is always open and awaits a sincere prayer from **a sincere heart**, key number three. Honesty and transparency are key ingredients that should undergird every prayer. Sincerity is God's expectation of our prayers. Psalm 17:1-5 is a sincere prayer that I want to highlight.

> Hear me, LORD, my plea is just; listen to my cry. Hear my prayer—it does not rise from deceitful lips. Let my vindication come from you; may your eyes see what is right. Though you probe my heart, though you examine me at night and test me, you will find that I have planned no evil; my mouth has not transgressed. Though people tried to bribe me, I have kept myself from the ways of the

violent through what your lips have commanded. My steps have held to your paths; my feet have not stumbled.

Sincerity clearly must be free of deceit and dishonesty, so it will penetrate the heart of God. Augustine of Hippo, the great Christian theologian of the fourth and fifth centuries, strengthens my argument about the importance of a sincere heart. He says that prayer must be "counterintuitive" based off truth that God dispenses "peace, happiness and consolation . . . only found in Christ" through prayer.[15] Further, Augustine asserted that "the scales had to come off the eyes" of the prayer warrior. These scales represent insincerity of heart, which will hamper prayers. This is like asking forgiveness, but not being sincere. This reminds me of a child who was told by his or her parents to apologize to a teacher for being disrespectful. The child offers an insincere apology just to appease his or her parents. This apology is insincere because the child's heart isn't into the apology.

As a child, I had a conversation with my cousin about the sincerity of prayer. I expressed that I wanted some superhero action figures to play with. I asked him, "How do I get these toys?" My cousin responded that I should pray and ask God to provide direction to my parents in terms of where to buy these toys. I still had some doubts about whether my wish would come to fulfillment. Sensing and responding to my doubts, my cousin said that I had to have a sincere heart when I approached God in prayer. Furthermore, he stressed to me that I needed to vocalize the importance of wanting the toy and that God would direct my parents accordingly. Though my example may seem trivial, it highlights the necessity for a sincere heart in prayer.

BIBLICAL EXAMPLE OF A SINCERE HEART

John 5:1-15 provides us with an eye-opening account of an individual with a sincere heart who sought the Lord. The story identifies an unnamed,

---

15 Philip Schaff, ed., *Nicene and Post-Nicene Fathers: First Series S014, Vol. 1*, Christian Classics Ethereal Library, Peabody, MA: Hendrickson Pub, 1887, pp. 997-1015.

paralyzed man who was stuck in the same miserable condition for thirty-eight years. For almost forty years, this man came to the pool of Bethesda, which is in the Holy City of Jerusalem, hoping to be healed. After not receiving his healing, frustration seems to set in; and as the man put it, "While I am trying to get in, someone else goes down ahead of me" (John 5:7). Clearly, this man's actions reflected his desire to be made whole. Judging by Jesus' response, it appeared that Jesus read this man's sincerity. "Then Jesus said to him, 'Get up! Pick up your mat and walk.' At once the man was cured; he picked up his mat and walked." Jesus rewarded this man for his sincerity.

The Good News is that the miracle performed in the life of this man is also available to us. Daily, the Lord examines our hearts to ensure that we are sincere. When God looks at our hearts and sees sincerity, God will meet our needs according to His plans (Romans 8:28). Just like Jesus assessed the sincerity of the man's heart, he also looks at the genuineness of our hearts and will do what needs to be done in our lives.

The other part of his sincerity that sticks out is his determination to be healed. For thirty-eight years, this gentleman still went to the pool, hoping to be healed. Sincerity and determination go together like butter on toast, as we need both to thrive in life. Our sincerity is often measured through our determination. How bad do we want to grow in Christian maturity? How bad do we want to be delivered from a bad habit?

It is imperative for us to have a sincere heart when we have offended someone and need to apologize. When we say unkind things, we need to go to the one that we offended and say that we are sorry. When we apologize, we must have a sincere heart, or it will appear to the other party that we don't have any real contrition. As a result, the person will not feel better as a result of our apology. This insincerity is the reason why so many broken relationships exist.

In synopsis, sincerity is a prerequisite for a powerful prayer life. God must know that we mean our prayers. God must know that our petitions are important to us. God must know that we are genuine in our approach to God in prayer. Sincerity is needed in our prayer life. We need to be honest and upfront with God. We don't need any ulterior motives, which may hinder our prayers. God examines and looks for a sincere heart.

KEY #4: A SEEKER MINDSET

"Look to the LORD and his strength; seek his face always" (1 Chronicles 16:11).

Imagine searching for a misplaced cell phone. Generally, you look in the places where you usually keep the phone. This may be your pocket or a drawer. Ladies and gentlemen, this continual quest to locate the cell phone illustrates a seeker mindset, which means that you will search for the object until you find it.

Key number four is we must approach prayer with a **seeker mindset.** This simply means that when we pray, we must have an attitude of searching the heart and mind of God. A seeker mindset is the approach that King David took as he prayed in Psalm 63. This psalm is on the heels of some of David's tumultuous life events—being devalued by his father, Jesse, and the prophet Samuel (1 Samuel 16:7); his affair with Bathsheba in 2 Samuel 11 and 2 Samuel 21:5; and his battle with his enemy, the Philistines (Psalm 3:7). As a result of these incidents, David needs forgiveness (Psalm 57), deliverance (Psalm 59), and help (Psalm 61). Read these poetic words: "You, God, are my God, earnestly I seek you; I thirst for you, my whole being longs for you, in a dry and parched land where there is no water" (Psalm 63:1). His words are piercing and paint a clear picture of his desire and dependence on the presence of God to sustain him. He realized that he needed God through every moment of life.

Psalm 63 poignantly reveals that David wholeheartedly sought the Lord with every ounce of his being. This meant that his mind, energy, and will were centered on God's plan for his life. Like David, we need to seek God like our lives depend on it.

A succinct statement on prayer is found in Matthew 7:7 and Luke 11:9, where it says, "Ask and it will be given to you; seek and you will find; knock and the door will be opened to you." This is a process of action to seek God. Seeking, asking, and knocking depict an active prayer life.

ILLUSTRATION

As a boy, I use to play hide and seek with my friends in my dark basement. I fervently searched throughout my basement and looked in the bathroom and in every room for my friends. I would listen for noises and would look for movement that would clue me in to their whereabouts. I only searched in the basement for my friends because I knew they weren't in another location. Finding my friends was always fulfilling as I felt a sense of accomplishment.

In the same manner, when we search for God, we will have a sense of achievement. We don't have to search for God in shallow relationships and material possessions that lead nowhere. We can search for God in prayer and experience wholeness. We just must remember that seeking God is a conscious effort. As believers, we should aim to "set [our] mind[s] on things above" (Colossians 3:2). Our attention needs to be on God.

The second part of a seeker mindset is having a life that aligns with God's plans. This means to focus on "things above" (Gal. 5:22-23), which are "the fruit of the Spirit . . . love, joy, peace, forbearance, kindness, goodness, faithfulness, gentleness and self-control." These fruits represent the aspects that satisfy the Lord. These are not selfishness and self-serving in nature.

NO TIMEFRAMES

Additionally, seeking God doesn't mean putting timeframes on God. This means not restricting God to act or move when we want God to move. Conversely, the Lord will move when He is ready to act. Ecclesiastes 3:1 puts it this way: "There is a time for everything, and a season for every activity under the heavens." This means that God does things in His time. Notice that the writer of the book of Ecclesiastes never mentions his expectation for God to intercede and intervene at a time.

Not knowing the timeframes is difficult for us as we desire to know the details of our situations. We want to know when we will start a family. We want to know when we will receive our healing. We want to know when we would meet that special someone with whom we will spend the rest of our lives. As humans, we want to know the details of our lives. On the other hand, being near God helps us behave in a positive way and embodies being in God's presence.

Being near God helps us behave in a positive way and embodies being in God's presence. So, the seeker asks God, "What is Your will for my life? What should I do in this situation? How can I deal with the trying times in my life?" These are questions that will come from the heart and mouth of one who seeks guidance from the Lord.

TRANSACTIONAL PRAYER

Conversely, to a seeker mindset is transactional prayer. Unfortunately, some treat God like an ATM and only seek the Lord when they want or need something. After they pray and get what they want, they go about their way. They may not even think about God again until they have another need. This superficial prayer life is self-serving and non-relational and diminishes the true relational nature of prayer.

Transactional prayer also tells God that He is only an emergency option. How do we think that makes God feel? God does not desire to be our last option when things get hard but wants to be the first Name that we call upon in every matter.

Another component of transactional prayer is bargaining. Bargaining means to negotiate. One that bargains may say, "God, I promise to follow You if You bless me with the new car stereo." And in this scenario, the individual has no intention of following God. This prayer doesn't signify that one is interested in coming closer to the Lord, but rather that they want the material possession.

Regrettably, this transactional nature of prayer also takes place in relationships. When the foundation of our relationships is solely based on gain, they usually won't last. One party in the relationship usually feels used and unappreciated, which ends the relationship. This self-centered mindset causes separation and divorce. Often, one-sided relationships will come to an end.

God is concerned with the spirit behind our prayers and our attitudes. It is important to highlight that seeking is a constant process. It is not a one-time event, but a continual experience. Believer in Christ, seeking the Lord will bring fulfillment to our lives. Seeking the Lord will always lead us in the right direction, which doesn't mean that everything will run smoothly, but that it will be right.

KEY # 5: WAIT FOR GOD'S RESPONSE

"Be still before the Lord and wait patiently for him" (Psalm 37:7).

We have all probably had to wait in long grocery store lines to purchase our groceries. Sometimes, the wait seems like an eternity. However, the customer must be willing to wait until they are able to pay for their items. There are times waiting is necessary to accomplish our endeavors.

Key number five is that we must **wait for God's response.** What good is it to speak to God and not wait for God's response? Ponder this thought for a moment. When you ask someone a question, you should wait for their response. Whether that is in a face-to-face conversation, via telephone, or through a text message, you need to wait for a response.

Waiting on God is like waiting for an internet connection which reminds us of the patience needed for a wireless connection. A few days ago, I sat in my home and didn't have access to my internet. I had to see if turning off and restarting my computer would fix my problem. It did.

When speaking to the Creator of the universe, the least we should do is to wait for God to respond. This means when we ask God for direction on any matter, we should wait. For example, if one is asking for God's guidance in choosing a mate, he or she should wait until God gives clarity. My meaning is that we need to wait for a move from God. Now, God's response may be through non-verbal communication, such as receiving or not receiving employment or hearing godly advice from friends. God will answer in one way or another.

BIBLICAL EXAMPLE OF WAITING ON GOD

The Israelites' journey toward the Promised Land is an example of waiting on God. Joshua 5:6 lets us know that the Israelites were in the wilderness for forty years prior to entering the Promised Land. While the Israelites were in the wilderness, Moses continued to pray and wait on the Lord (Exodus 32:9-14). And they finally entered the Promised Land after this long wait.

The moral of this story is that we must continue to turn to God in our time of waiting. It may take a while before God brings our breakthrough but hold on to God's unchanging hand. Continue to seek God. This account in the Old Testament teaches that blessings and rewards come from patience; so, keep waiting on God.

Waiting on God's response means waiting for a Divine confirmation to our requests. Here is an example to demonstrate what waiting on God looks like: A godly man may be in love with a woman. He is attracted to the young lady's intelligence, Christian spirit, personality, and beauty. He begins to question whether he should propose to the lady. He wants some validation that this is the woman whom God intends for him to spend the rest of his life with as his wife. He begins to study the Scriptures and comes across the passage in Galatians 3:22, which talks about the fruit of the Spirit being love, joy, and peace. He also sees that she is the virtuous woman discussed in Proverbs 31. He realizes that his girlfriend possesses these attributes and comes to the realization that her traits align with the Scriptures. This young man waited on the Lord to see what God thought about his interest to marry this woman.

GOD WAITS ON US

I would be remiss if I didn't mention that sometimes, God waits on us before He will move. God waits for us to take the necessary step toward the Him before He will act. Let's look at the account of Jonah. Jonah was called to Nineveh to preach against the city (Jonah 1:2). Sadly, he didn't go and went to Tarshish instead (Jonah 1:3). Due to his disobedience, he ended up in the belly of a fish (Jonah 1:17). While in the belly of the fish, Jonah began to pray. During his prayer, he had a change of heart and decided to go to Nineveh as directed (Jonah 2:1-9). After he made the decision to go, God allowed him to escape the belly of the fish (Jonah 2:10). Jonah went to Nineveh (Jonah 3:3); and because of Jonah's obedience, the people of Nineveh repented, and God decided not to destroy Nineveh (Jonah 3:10).

This account of Jonah provides us with a compelling story that teaches us that God will wait on humans to be obedient. God already revealed God's plan to Jonah, but Jonah disregarded it and did his own thing. God could have helped Jonah out of the belly of the fish sooner but waited for Jonah to follow the Lord's plan instead.

WHAT HAPPENS WHEN WE DON'T WAIT?

"Be patient, then, brothers and sisters, until the Lord's coming. See how the farmer waits for the land to yield its valuable crop, patiently waiting for the autumn and spring rains" (James 5:7).

The book of Exodus presents us with a timely example of the consequences for impatience. Moses, the great Hebrew leader, was told by God to "speak to that rock," which would provide water (Numbers 20:8). Lamentably, he impatiently struck the rock to get the water because of his anger toward the Israelites (Numbers 20:11). As a result, God prohibited Moses from entering the Promised Land with the other Hebrews (Numbers 20:12). Yes, Moses—the same man who demonstrated unparalleled courage by helping the Israelites escape from 430 years of slavery (Exodus 12:40)—would not step foot on the soil of the Promised Land because of his impatience, which led to disobedience. Impatience keeps us from our blessings.

At times, we run into self-inflicted heartbreaks and disappointments because we refuse to wait on God. We are impulsive and make hasty decisions. Admittedly, we are all guilty of being impatient at times. Let's face it, we live in an instant gratification society, and we want things to happen right way. In our lives, we want to financially prosper, get out of debt, and not have to deal with pain. Often, we grow impatient when these issues aren't immediately resolved, but we must wait on God.

How do we think that makes God feel when we won't wait for His response? God may feel that we don't value Him enough to take time and listen for a response. In these instances, our prayers are baseless and empty because we are not willing to wait on the Lord.

ILLUSTRATION

Three years ago, I drove to work and noticed an impatient driver tailing my vehicle. As I drove on the bridge, the driver continued to drive within inches of my car. Finally, she got in front of me and weaved in and out of traffic. The driver quickly darted into the right lane, but it appeared that she didn't take the time to look to see there was a car in that lane. Regrettably, the result was an accident at the bottom of the bridge. This accident could have been avoided if the driver recognized another vehicle and patiently waited for the other vehicle to pass her.

In our prayer lives, we must be willing to wait on God because God will lead us to what is best for us. God knows what is in our best interest. It is good to know that the God of creation is in our corner.

Additionally, following God's will helps us escape the avoidable disappointments in our lives. This is because God will lead us in the right direction, which will help us avoid some possible detours in life. We may be able to avoid unnecessary drama. The previous example of Moses is an unnecessary disappointment because of his disobedience. The take-home point is that when we don't follow behind God, we may miss out on a blessing.

Waiting is a two-way street. It involves us waiting on God, and sometimes, God waits on us. God wants us to walk in obedience during our waiting. Waiting on God will save us from some emotional scars and bruises as we won't rush to make rash decisions which get us in trouble. Waiting includes not going against God and giving into frustration but does keep us safe.

KEY # 6: LISTEN

"My sheep listen to my voice; I know them, and they follow me" (John 10:27).

Key number six is **listening.** We must be willing to listen for and to God. Both are equally important in our prayer journey because our attention is set on the Lord. Before I proceed, I want to differentiate between listening and hearing.

Listening involves responding appropriately to what we hear. Parents tell their child not to put his or her hands on a hot stove, or the child will be burned. So, a child who is listening to their parents will not put their hands on a hot stove because he or she knows he or she will be burned. Using the same analogy, the child that only hears his or her parents' instructions may still put their hands on the hot stove and get burned. So, listening is a two-way street, and hearing means that words go in one ear and out the other. God listens to our requests, so we need to listen to God's response.

Here is a practical example of listening. I am portraying a customer who calls a local restaurant to place a carry out order below.

>Customer: Hello, I would like to place an order for food.
>Restaurant Representative: How may I help you?
>Customer: I would like to order a Caesar Salad and water.
>Restaurant Representative: Is there anything else?
>Customer: No, thank you!
>Restaurant Representative: I just want to make sure that I got your order right. Would you like a Caesar Salad and water?
>Customer: Yes, that is it.
>Restaurant Representative: That will be ten dollars, and your order will be ready in twenty minutes.
>Customer: Thank you!

We can see from this short skit that listening involves processing what the other person says. The restaurant representative made sure that he understood what the customer ordered. He did this by repeating the order to the customer. The customer verified the order, which confirmed in the mind of the restaurant representative that he had the order right. This is what listening entails—questions and confirmation.

LISTENING FOR GOD

Listening for God is the precondition to listening to God. One must listen, knowing that God has responded before he or she is able to comprehend what God says. In other words, when we pray, we should expect that God will speak to us. This act of listening to God is like an individual awaiting an important phone call. The waiting individual will keep the phone nearby as he or she waits for the call.

My point is that listening for God requires intentionality. It means that we desire to listen to God. We purpose in our hearts that God will speak, and we are ready to listen. This means going to a designated place, where we expect to meet God. This may be before work, going into the cafeteria early before your day gets started. This may be in the car while running errands. This is a time set aside to listen for God.

Sometimes, listening for God may involve us not speaking any words to God. This may come as a surprise to you, but you do not have to speak any words to God for God to speak to you. You would be amazed at how many times I find myself sitting still, and God reveals stuff to me that I previously questioned God about.

We must be willing to listen and not speak. We must be willing to let God speak. Scripture teaches us to be "slow to speak" (James 1:19). Here are two examples of listening for God in the Scriptures.

OLD TESTAMENT EXAMPLE

An Old Testament illustration of listening for God comes to us in Exodus 19. Moses and the Israelites just escaped the clutches of the Egyptians and were in the wilderness. It appears that Moses wanted clarity as to how to journey through the wilderness to get into the Promised Land. Look at how Moses listens for God. Exodus 19:3a says, "Then Moses went up to God." In other words, Moses approached God. Notice this passage doesn't say that Moses spoke to God. Instead, he went to God with the intent to listen to God. Moses went up to hear God's message for him to communicate to the

Israelites. This message gave Moses clear direction as to leading the Israelites to the Promised Land.

Later in the passage, we find that God did speak to Moses. God gave Moses the words to deliver to the Israelites. In other terms, God wanted Moses to reiterate to the Israelites His track record of delivering Israel from the Egyptian oppressors. Further, God said He would make the people of Israel a "treasured possession" if they followed Him (Exodus 19:5).

Listening for God is the preparatory act in a prayer before listening to God. It is a form of waiting for God. We must listen *for* God before we are able to listen *to* God. The Old and New Testament examples provide us with patriarchs who listened for God.

In Psalm 61—a psalm that was discussed earlier—David appeared to listen for God as he was running away from his enemies. He wanted to hear from God as he indicated in Psalm 61:1: "Hear my cry, O God; listen to my prayer." David took the time to wait for God before he moved.

NEW TESTAMENT EXAMPLE

In the New Testament, Jesus appeared to go to places of solitude to pray so that He would be able to listen for God on what God may say on a matter. In Luke 11:1, Jesus prayed "in a certain place."

After Jesus' prayer, He taught His disciples how to pray the Lord's Prayer (Matt. 6:9-13, Luke 11:1-4). What this teaches is that Jesus had to be in a space where He could understand and reflect on God during prayer. What Jesus did was listen for God.

LISTENING TO GOD

During our time of waiting, we need to listen to the Lord. This means adhering to what God says. Listening is what we should do when we wait on God. There is an old saying that says, "God gave us two ears and one month;

so, God must have meant for us to do twice as much listening as talking." And to listen, we must have our ears open to the voice of God.

One example of someone listening to God is found in Matthew 2:13-23. The angel of the Lord reveals to Joseph that he, Mary, and baby Jesus should flee to Egypt to escape King Herod, who would kill the infant Jesus. Joseph immediately listens to God and saves his family from certain death.

BIBLICAL EXAMPLE OF LISTENING

"My dear brothers and sisters, take note of this: Everyone should be quick to listen" (James 1:19).

A biblical example of listening is Mary, who received the exhilarating news from the angel of the Lord that she would become the mother of Jesus in Luke 1:26-38. Her response is striking. She didn't discredit, dispute, or discount the angel of the Lord because the message didn't make sense that a virgin would become pregnant and give birth. Instead, she accepted her responsibility. She also declared her obedience and did God's will. Fundamentally, she listened and believed the message.

For us to listen to God, we must recognize His voice. Sometimes, God speaks in an audible voice (Exodus 33:11), through other people and nature (1 Kings 19:12-13), or through an angel (Luke 1:26-38). God spoke to the people of Israel through prophets (Numbers 12:6-14) and in visions and dreams (Exodus 3:2-3; Job 33:15). The Scripture bears witness to the fact that God only speaks in line with His Word.

ILLUSTRATION

A common trait of a good therapist is that he or she listens to his or her clients. The therapist will not give feedback without first listening to the client. Listening is what helps the therapist make suggestions. For instance, a therapist will not realize that a client has issues with unforgiveness until the therapist listens to the client speak about the anger that still festers in his or her life.

For a therapist, listening also involves paying attention to the tone and body language. The therapist is studying the tone and body language to better understand the feelings that the client has. For instance, if a client has clenched fists and a negative facial expression whenever the individual speaks about his or her dad, that tips the therapist off to the fact that the client may have some resentment.

The client should listen to the suggestions from the therapist. Listening helps the client gain understanding in reference to the ideas he or she may have about his or her dad. In 1 Kings 19, God counsels Elijah because fear seized and held such a tight grip on him after he received a death threat from Jezebel that he didn't want to live any longer. In fact, he fled from his duties as a prophet and retreated to Mount Horeb. During his time in isolation, the Lord visited him and listened to his complaint. "'I have had enough, LORD,' he said. 'Take my life; I am no better than my ancestors." As Elijah was at this very low point, the Lord listened to his pain and told him to "get up and eat" (1 Kings 19:5). God told Elijah it was time to move on.

One of the many hats that God wears is that of a therapist. God helps us to navigate our feelings to His loving care. In addition, God wants to stabilize and strengthen us emotionally through listening to what is on our minds. Psalm 18 depicts the Lord in the role of a therapist. David vents before the Lord and makes known his misgivings. "The cords of death entangled me; the torrents of destruction overwhelmed me. The cords of the grave coiled around me; the snares of death confronted me" (Psalm 18:4-5). Specifically, he was afraid because his life was in danger. King Saul attempted to kill him, and he was on the run. To make matters worse, he had enemies who wanted him dead. Despite this tempestuous time, he prayed this remarkable psalm, and God responded in favor by sparing his life.

Remember that God may take on the role of a therapist in our lives. Like a therapist examines the body language of his or her client, God inspects our attitudes during prayer, and God wants to hear what is on our minds.

In summary, when God speaks, we need to listen. We need to pay attention to the commands of God, which will protect us. We should remember that God wants to hear and attend to us according to God's will.

WHEN GOD SAYS YES

"He will call on me, and I will answer him; I will be with him in trouble, I will deliver him and honor him" (Psalm 91:15).

When God says yes, amazing things happen. The bottom line is that transformational and life-altering changes begin to take shape in our lives. David sang this song in recognition of the Lord's deliverance of him from his enemies in 2 Samuel 22:1. In other words, God said yes to the idea of David being safe and so David emerged from the event unscathed.

In 1 Samuel 19, King David had his back against the wall as King Saul moved on him with a plot to kill him. As David was on the verge of death, he called on the Lord for direction. The Lord provided him a way of escape from Saul. David emerged from this event with a confident calmness as he continued to serve God.

There are times that we do not know how to react in the right manner when God says yes. We respond to God with doubt and unbelief. God may have answered a prayer request of old, and we are still unable to accept that God has granted our request for one reason or another. Acts 12 records Peter being set free from prison. What is interesting is that the church prayed for his release (Acts 12:5). Next, the unthinkable happens, and Peter is released from prison (Acts 12:6-7). Rhoda, one of the members of the house, answers the door and, to her surprise, finds Peter standing in front of her (Acts 12:13). When she shares the news with the others, their response is disbelief: "You're out of your mind" (Acts 12:15). Upon his release, you would think they would believe the report that he was free, but they succumb to doubt. It was only when they looked and saw Peter that they believed that he was released from prison.

When God says yes, be prepared to embrace the blessing. Instead of allowing fear and doubt to seize and control your thinking, try to be ecstatic. Follow Rhoda's example in the above text and tell friends and others about how God has answered your prayers.

WHEN GOD SAYS NO

> "But because of you the LORD was angry with me and would not listen to me. 'That is enough,' the LORD said. 'Do not speak to me anymore about this matter'" (Deuteronomy 3:26).

Sometimes, we may wonder why our prayers are not being answered. In fact, God may flatly deny our requests. We are not alone, as God has said no to even the most faithful of the Bible.

The Bible offers a riveting example of God's denial of King David. In 2 Samuel 7, we read that David wanted to build the temple of the Lord. Mentally and emotionally, he prepared and planned to build this temple to demonstrate his appreciation of God. He wanted to build God this lavish home and had all the right intentions to build the temple. Yet, God did not grant him his heart's desire because God had an alternate plan.

God's plan was for Solomon, David's son, to build the temple, as stated in 2 Samuel 7:12: "When your days are over and you rest with your ancestors, I will raise up your offspring to succeed you, your own flesh and blood, and I will establish his kingdom." In other words, God told David no.

Though David's situation is not exactly a prayer, it was his wish that I want to focus on. David's longing was to build a special type of structure, which would serve as the dwelling place for the living God. He wanted to construct something that was on a grand scale for the Creator. Nevertheless, God didn't share David's wish.

Applying the lesson from David to our own prayer lives, we learn that desire is often the origin of our prayers. We want something to come to fruition. Some common desires like making new friends and wise personal or business decisions are things that drive our prayers. They cause us to pray because we realize that for these things to come to reality, we need Divine regulation and involvement.

HOW SHOULD WE HANDLE GOD SAYING NO?

> *"And pray in the Spirit on all occasions with all kinds of prayers and requests. With this in mind, be alert and always keep on praying for all the Lord's people"* (Ephesians 6:18).

We may handle God telling us no through prayer and praise. Look at David's response to the news that he would not build the temple. He offers a prayer of praise to the Lord. Let David's words penetrate your heart: "But God said to me, 'You are not to build a house for my Name, because you are a warrior and have shed blood.' Yet the Lord, the God of Israel, chose me from my whole family to be king over Israel forever. He chose Judah as leader, and from the tribe of Judah he chose my family, and from my father's sons he was pleased to make me king over all Israel" (1 Chronicles 28:3-4).

Clearly, David got the message that he wasn't the one to build the temple. He allowed God's will to infiltrate his heart, and he articulated this prayer of acceptance to the will of God. His desire was pushed to the backseat, and he was okay with that. In fact, his attention shifted to the House of the Lord and not his selfish will to build the temple.

Yet, we witness David praising the Lord after God denied his request. He uplifted the name of the Lord instead of holding his head down. First Chronicles 29:10-20 is a song of praise to God. I will focus on verses ten and sixteen from this passage as they relate to how we handle God telling us no

Verse ten says, "David praised the LORD in the presence of the whole assembly, saying, 'Praise be to you, LORD, the God of our father Israel, from everlasting to everlasting." Verse sixteen says, "Lord our God, all this abundance that we have provided for building you a temple for your Holy Name comes from your hand, and all of it belongs to you."

David focused on praising the Lord instead of his heartbreak. What a valuable lesson for each of us to concentrate on listening to God instead of our feelings. Focusing on the Lord will help us handle when God says no because we know that God has something greater in store for us. Some of us may pray that we build buildings or become best-selling authors, but God may say no. God may have someone else in our family accomplish our dreams, or a friend may complete the project that we want to do. During these times, we shouldn't get upset with God. On the contrary, we need to keep in mind that God has a plan and purpose.

WHEN NO MEANS NOT NOW

"But God said to me, 'You are not to build a house for my Name, because you are a warrior and have shed blood'" (1 Chronicles 28:3).

Continuing with the above biblical reference, we learn that God's no to David didn't mean that He didn't want the temple to be built, but that God didn't want the temple to be built *at that time*. The point is that the "not now" was all about God's perfect timing. God wanted Solomon, a man of peace, to build the temple instead of David, a man of war. Solomon, the architect of the temple, made a spotless structure when God wanted the building to be constructed (1 Kings 6).

The same is true in our lives. Sometimes, God tells us not now. Maybe, you desire to have the higher paying job or to move into a new neighborhood, but God says not now. During these times, we must not get discouraged, but be encouraged to do God's will.

Instead of being bitter by the fact that he wasn't building the temple, David collected supplies for this holy edifice to help Solomon (1 Chronicles 22:14-16). He wasn't discouraged that God didn't want him to build the temple but was excited that God would finally have an appropriate dwelling place. David was enthusiastic that the plan of the Lord would come into being.

The key to understanding the meaning of the "not now" moments in our lives is a willingness to listen to God. David willingly listened to the Lord. He didn't hold onto his personal longing to build the temple above God's plan and purpose. Instead, he continued to fulfill his God-given responsibilities and ungrudgingly served as king (1 Chronicles 22:17-19).

Not now is not the end of the world. It means that we must wait until God brings His purpose into execution. Just like the construction of the temple, God may have a future timeline for something we yearn to come to realization, but we just must wait.

Our attitudes should reflect that we listen to God. David had a positive disposition because he accepted God's purpose and plan for the construction of the temple. He understood that life did not always go according to his plans, but always were part of God's will. Therefore, he never allowed ambition to dictate or distract him from governing the people of Israel.

Listening for God sets the stage for us to listen to God. We must keep our eyes open to the move of God. This means when we pray, we need to anticipate a response from the Lord. That means we must believe that God will not be silent on our behalf. On the other hand, we must trust that God not only hears our cries, but that God will answer.

KEY # 7: PRAYING GOD'S WORD

"May these words of my mouth and this meditation of my heart be pleasing in your sight, LORD, my Rock and my Redeemer" (Psalm 19:14).

Last, but certainly not least, key number seven is that we need to pray God's Word to receive content for our prayers. We know that we are to pray for the hungry because of what is seen in Scripture when Jesus prays and feeds the hungry (Matthew 14:13-21; Mark 6:30-44; Luke 9:10-17; John 6:1-15). We know that we should pray for other Christians based on Ephesians 6:18. We know that we should pray for people to be in the truth because John 17:17 says, "Sanctify them by the truth; your word is truth."

The key point is that in order to pray God's Word, we must know God's Word. We must know what the Bible says about different subjects. We should know how God views relationships, the elderly, and environmental issues. This information will instruct our prayers.

Praying the Scriptures is a model seen throughout the Holy Bible. Moses made a plea for God's mercy in Exodus 34:6: "The LORD, the LORD, the compassionate and gracious God, slow to anger, abounding in love and faithfulness." The prophet Nehemiah quotes the passage in Nehemiah 9:17-18. The Gospel of Matthew shows Jesus speaking these words when He was dying on the cross; He prays this desperate prayer, quoting Psalm 22:1: "My God, my God, why have you forsaken me" (Matthew 27:46).

Praying God's Word kept Jesus aligned with the plans and purposes of God. He never lost track of His purpose for coming to Earth because of His amazing prayer life. Additionally, Jesus overcame His inner turmoil and anxiety by praying the Word of God.

Praying God's Word is like entering a password to enter a home. When a person enters his or her home, the alarm system will sound. Many times, it is a loud noise that will ensue until the password is entered. This is the case because the alarm system recognizes the alarm password. Similarly, when we pray God's Word, God recognizes the prayer and responds.

Before we can pray that God's will come to completion, we must know God's Word. We must study the Scriptures. Second Timothy 2:15 says, "Do your best to present yourself to God as one approved, a worker who does not need to be ashamed and who correctly handles the word of truth." We may present ourselves to the Lord by researching the Scriptures for answers and direction. This entails becoming learned in the Scripture. What do the Scriptures say about subjects? For instance, what does the Scripture say about helping the needy? What does the Bible teach in reference to how we treat others? These are questions that will reveal God's will.

PRAYING IN GOD'S WILL

"Your will be done" (Matthew 6:10).

Praying God's will must be the guiding principle behind our prayers for effective and purposeful prayer (James 4:15). A closer look at prayer in Scripture discloses that prayer should be lined up with God's will. First John 5:14 says, "This is the confidence we have in approaching God: that if we ask anything according to his will, he hears us." This means that whatever we pray, we should ask for the Lord's will to be done.

Let's look at King Solomon's prayer that aligned with God's will. The king sought wisdom and not wealth. Second Chronicles 1:11-12 says:

> God said to Solomon, "Since this is your heart's desire and you have not asked for wealth, possessions or honor, nor for the death of your enemies, and since you have not asked for a long life but for wisdom and knowledge to govern my people over whom I have made you king, therefore wisdom and knowledge will be given you. And I will also give you wealth, possessions and honor, such as no king who was before you ever had and none after you will have."

Praying in God's will involves exchanging our desires for God's. It is letting go of our control because we exchange our preference and wish for what God has planned for our lives. Therefore, praying the will of God expands and enriches us.

CHAPTER 7
PRAYER AND HEALTH

"And the prayer offered in faith will make the sick person well" (James 5:15).

In addition to experiencing power, there have been many psychological studies and scientific research that show that prayer improves health. I liken prayer to a spiritual cardiovascular exercise. It helps us through the demands in our lives. It gets us through seen and unseen adversity. Specifically, prayer reduces stress and anxiety. According to a recent *Huffington Post* article, prayer is the most common and frequently utilized alternative therapy in America today. "Over 85% of people that suffer a major illness pray."[16] This means that most people pray to address sickness.

The editorial also points out that this number is significantly higher than those who use alternative healing methods such as herbs and medication. Unlike herbs and medication, there are no side effects with prayer. Prayer won't make us lightheaded or drowsy like some over-the-counter medications. Nowhere in the Bible does it say that anyone will experience negative reactions due to prayer. What a blessing it is to be treated without the unwanted side effects.

The above paragraph verifies that through God, prayer strengthens the body. Just the fact that the movement of prayer makes a difference on our health speaks volumes. It means that it helps the body fight sickness. Just

---

[16] Richard Schiffman, "Why People Who Pray Are Healthier Than Those Who Don't," HuffingtonPost.com, http://www.huffingtonpost.com/richard-schiffman/why-people-who-pray-are-heathier_b_1197313.html (accessed September 17, 2016).

think about reasons that you go to the doctor: high blood pressure, aches and pains, or depression. If these risk factors aren't addressed, one may develop heart disease and can possibly die. I am not trying to scare you, but just want to mention this startling reality.

Stress is the chief culprit behind these inconveniences. What is stress? "Stress is the body's natural defense against predators and danger. It flushes the body with hormones to prepare systems to evade or confront danger. This is known as the 'fight-or-flight' mechanism."[17] In other words, stress is how our body and mind seek to protect themselves against external forces, such as a demanding job or health issues. Financial and medicals issues are some common stressors. Not having enough money to pay the bills and going to the doctor and getting a bad health report are things that stress us out.

How do we deal with these and other stressors? We must pray. Psalm 94:19 records a time of great anxiety for King David. He was stressed and besieged with worry and concern because Israel is oppressed by persecutors. He cries to the Lord with the following rousing words: "When anxiety was great within me, your consolation brought me joy." Consequently, David and Israel experienced victory in Psalm 118.

The epistle of James makes it abundantly clear that there is a relationship between prayer and health. We find these words in the letter pertaining to prayer and healing in James 5:14-15: "Is anyone among you sick? Let them call the elders of the church to pray over them and anoint them with oil in the name of the Lord. And the prayer offered in faith will make the sick person well; the Lord will raise them up. If they have sinned, they will be forgiven. This shows us the inextricable link between prayer and the healing of sickness, and that stress can be managed through prayer.

God increases our stamina through prayer. Therefore, prayer helps our bodies endure and grants us resilience. I go back to Jesus' awe-inspiring prayer

---

[17] Christian Nordqvist, "Why Stress Happens and How to Manage It," MedicalNewsToday.com, https://www.medicalnewstoday.com/articles/145855.php. (accessed on September 26, 2017).

on the cross in Luke 22:42: "Father, if you are willing, take this cup from me; yet not my will, but yours be done." This faint, but strong, prayer from Jesus is a prayer asking for stamina. He asked God to help Him during His time of immense weakness and pain on the cross.

Dr. Andrew Newberg, Director of the Center for Spirituality and the Mind at the University of Pennsylvania, conducted a study of Tibetan Buddhists in meditation and Franciscan nuns in prayer which showed comparable decreased activity in the parts of the brain that are associated with sense of self and spatial orientation in both groups. He also found that prayer and meditation increase levels of dopamine, which is associated with states of well-being and joy.[18] From reading Dr. Newberg's statement, prayer helps the mind and body to unwind by clearing up mental and emotional imbalance.

As a result of these disorders, some are ostracized and feel disconnected from others. Personal attacks and name-calling of individuals who suffer from these illnesses are common. Consequently, some may lose their drive for living or feel hopeless. Well, I just want to reassure and remind anyone who suffers or knows anyone who suffers from mental illness that God, through the conduit of prayer, will help manage the disorder.

EASING MY MIND

Humans were created for peace and harmony. From reading Genesis 2:8-12, we see a picture of peace and serenity in the Garden of Eden.

> Now the LORD God had planted a garden in the east, in Eden; and there he put the man he had formed. The LORD God made all kinds of trees grow out of the ground—trees that were pleasing to the eye and good for food. In the middle of the garden were the tree of life and the tree of the knowledge of good and evil. A river watering the garden flowed from Eden; from there it

---

[18] Richard Schiffman, "Why People Who Pray Are Healthier Than Those Who Don't," HuffingtonPost.com, http://www.huffingtonpost.com/richard-schiffman/why-people-who-pray-are-heathier_b_1197313.html (accessed September 17, 2016).

was separated into four headwaters. The name of the first is the Pishon; it winds through the entire land of Havilah, where there is gold. (The gold of that land is good; aromatic resin and onyx are also there.)

Therefore, when we pray, we are able to be restored mentally, emotionally, and physically to our original state. God uses this channel of prayer to bring that calming presence to us.

DEPRESSION

Depression is lasting sadness. With that said, depression is a multilayered condition that affects many people. For the sake of this manuscript, I will lightly touch on different forms of depression—which include Persistent Depressive Disorder, Perinatal Depression, Psychotic Depression, Seasonal Affective Disorder, and Bipolar Disorder. Each alters the mood and creates a state of mental and emotional gloominess. For the purposes of this work, I will limit my discussion to Psychotic Depression, Seasonal Affective Disorder, and Bipolar Disorder as I have encountered and worked with people with these disorders.

Psychotic Depression is a type of major depression that may manifest in the forms of hallucinations or delusions. This means imaging things that are not real. Sudden and unusual outbursts are traits that individuals with Psychotic Depression display.

"Seasonal Affective Disorder is a type of depression that's related to changes in seasons—SAD begins and ends at about the same times every year. If you're like most people with SAD, your symptoms start in the fall and continue into the winter months; sapping your energy and making you feel moody."[19] This condition is not as strong during the summer and the spring months while the sun stays out longer. With this disorder, temperatures and the presence or the absence of the sun will dictate a person's mood.

---
19 "Seasonal affective disorder (SAD)," MayoClinic.com, https://www.mayoclinic.org/diseases-conditions/seasonal-affective-disorder/symptoms-causes/syc-20364651. (accessed May 29, 2019).

"Bipolar disorder (once known as manic depression or manic-depressive disorder) causes serious shifts in mood, energy, thinking, and behavior—from the highs of mania on one extreme, to the lows of depression on the other. More than just a fleeting good or bad mood, the cycles of bipolar disorder last for days, weeks, or months."[20] This is sustained depression.

The non-clinical definition of depression is changes in the brain. Specifically, these are chemical changes and imbalances in the brain. Therefore, it is important to clear any misnomers about depression. Depression is not because of spiritual failure. It is not due to a character flaw, but it is a mental disorder.

Before I move forward, if you know anyone that expresses suicidal ideations or threatens to harm someone else, please get help. In the United States, please do not hesitate to call 911, or The National Helpline is a great resource for those experiencing a mental health crisis and substance abuse. They can be reached 24/7 and 365 days a year at 1-800-662-4357. In the United Kingdom, a mental health crisis resource is Shout. "Text SHOUT to 85258 from anywhere in the UK, anytime, about any type of crisis."[21]

These different forms of depression are serious. They negatively impact people and can suck the very life out of individuals. How do you deal with depression in a healthy manner so that you do not get stuck in a rut?

TREATMENT FOR ILLNESS

Antidepressants are the type of medication that is used to treat these mental health challenges. Many people take daily medications to help manage their condition. Quality sleep, clarity of mind, and improved bodily functions are some of the distinct ways that antidepressants help treat mental illness. According to www.helpguide.org, a trusted mental and emotional health guide, research also points out that most people don't become symptom-free

---

20 Melinda Smith, M.A. and Jeanne Segal, Ph.D, "Bipolar Disorder Signs and Symptoms," https://www.helpguide.org/articles/bipolar-disorder/bipolar-disorder-signs-and-symptoms.htm. (accessed on May 30, 2019).
21 "Shout," Crisistextline, https://www.crisistextline.uk. (accessed July 12, 2019).

as a result of taking antidepressants. The same website highlights that there are associated side effects with antidepressants that may cause an individual to sweat and have a dry mouth. These affects may cause discomfort in an individual, but I want to reintroduce to you an always reliable treatment for mental health illness: prayer.

PRAYER AND MEDICATION

A benefit of prayer is that we can never overdose because we can never pray too much for our situation. So, if we are feeling down, we may constantly pray and experience healing instead of bodily harm. You may never become unconscious or die because of prayer, which cannot be said about overdosing on medication. Some have taken too much medication to bury their pain. Unfortunately, this unhealthy and self-injurious behavior can be life-threatening. Conversely, we are implored to "pray continually" (1 Thessalonians 5:17). This means that prayer never hurts, but only helps us.

I know the above definitions may sound grim but hold on. God may offer a new lease on life as it pertains to mental health illness through prayer. Through prayer, God massages our spirit and soothes our restlessness. The good news is that the Bible gives us a story about God using prayer to help one through a mental health crisis.

EXAMPLE FROM 1 KINGS 19

Earlier, I mentioned the Hebrew prophet Elijah's bout with depression. He seemed to experience symptoms of psychotic depression. He was weary and retreated to a cave, feverishly afraid. His life was threatened by Jezebel. He even asked God to take his life. Yet, at this very low point in his life, he spoke to the Lord. God flipped the script and encouraged him by enlarging his responsibilities as the one who would anoint two prophets (v. 15-16) Elijah went on to be one of the trailblazers in Jewish history. He displayed tremendous faith and stood against the prevalent idol worship (1 Kings 18:18). Through prayer, God lifted Elijah's spirits and strengthened him to move past his agony. He left the cave and continued as a prophet.

Elijah gives us a commanding illustration about the power of God through prayer over depression. Depression weighed Elijah down, but God lifted him from his fog. Elijah's heartfelt prayer gave him strength.

Prayer was the medicine that Elijah needed to survive. This medicine fueled him to minister to the Jewish community at the time.

A PERSONAL PRAYER TESTIMONY

During my senior year of high school, I dealt with some anxiety and unsettledness as I did not know if any colleges would accept me. I didn't have the highest grades and had a low SAT score. When I received multiple rejection letters, I was heartbroken. Almost every day for over a month, I checked the mail to see if any colleges had sent acceptance letters to me. I began to feel discouraged and started wondering if I would go to college. I began doing the only thing that I knew would make a difference—pray. Every evening following swim practice, I would pray during my drive home and would call out to the Lord and tell Him about my heartache. I expressed to God that I started doubting my intellect and if it was God's plan for me to attend college. Peaceful sensations flooded my being during and after the prayer time. As a result, the sometimes-stressful drive became pleasant and enjoyable. Additionally, I was able to rest well at night, though I hadn't been accepted by any colleges. A couple of months later, God answered my prayer. I got an acceptance letter from Frostburg State University; but more importantly, I learned the value of persistent prayer.

In fact, there are proven strategies that help people address their mental health issues. From reading an article from *Everyday Health*, I identified ways that prayer relieves stress in the life of a person. The following are often found in stress management techniques. These ways include a broader sense of purpose, boosted morale, social interaction, and exercise.

BROADER SENSE OF PURPOSE

God uses prayer to gives us a broader sense of purpose because we acknowledge that there is a Higher Power. Since there is a Supernatural Power, we shouldn't be self-consumed, but must shift our focus to God. With God as the focal point in our lives, we start to think about what pleases the Lord and our purpose for living (Romans 8:28 and Ephesians 5:10).

Through prayer, God reveals our purpose. Remember when Moses went to Mount Sinai, where he prayed to the Lord and received the Ten Commandments (Exod. 34:28-29)? During Moses' prayer time with God, God revealed that Moses would be the liberator of the Israelites (Exodus 4:10-11). God gave Moses a renewed sense of purpose, which gave him the needed hope to lead the Israelites to freedom. Prior to this revelation, Moses was an outcast, not accepted by the Jewish people or the Egyptians (Exodus 2:14-21). He was a recluse and didn't feel that he belonged to any group.

God also uses prayer to expose our purpose in our pain. Look at these touching words from Jesus to convey His God-appointed purpose in spite of His painful death on the cross: "Father, if you are willing, take this cup from me; yet not my will, but yours be done" (Luke 22:42). What we learn from Jesus' profound words is that sometimes, our prayer needs to be that God changes us and not our circumstances. In other words, our outer circumstances may not get better, but God will equip us to handle the situation because we constantly remember what our purpose is in life.

BOOSTED MORALE

God uses prayer to boost morale. When we stop thinking about our situations and lay our concerns at the feet of the Lord, we can breathe easi

This helps people overcome feeling weighed down from the cares of life. The strain of life is lifted, and we can experience serenity and calm in our lives. Therefore, our morale is lifted, and individuals can complete their daily tasks with vigor and a positive attitude.

A great example of prayer-boosting morale is seen in the life of Elijah (1 Kings 19). When Elijah went to Mount Horeb, as previously mentioned, he felt dismal and miserable about the place he had found himself. He was besieged and burdened with trepidation as his life was in jeopardy. However, as he prayed, his morale boosted, and he suddenly became optimistic and began to do the work of the Lord. This swift shift in focus may be attributed to the work of God through prayer because his mind was cleared, and he was able to focus on God's plan for his life. This focus enabled him to move forward.

It appears that prayer shifts our focus from our problem to the presence of God, which leads to a morale boost. We begin to think about God and less about our problems. Like Elijah, we can think about the possibilities that God will intercede in our situations. We are replacing negative thoughts with positive thoughts, which uplift our spirits.

SOCIAL INTERACTION

A seminal aspect of depression is the desire to be isolated from others. Depression can separate us from others and lead us to a dark place of sorrow. I recall going through a period of depression while I studied at Candler School of Theology during my first year. Seven hundred miles from home, I struggled to find companionship and felt depressed because I didn't have my family and friends nearby. I recall sitting in darkness one Friday evening, wishing that I had someone to spend quality time with. I needed social interaction to help me through my loneliness.

Social interaction is simply coming together. It validates one's feelings and affirms one's choices. This peer interaction can help one overcome the feelings of sadness, depression, and despair. As I made more friends, my depression subsided because I felt valued and connected.

OUTWARD MOVEMENT

Corporate prayer (individuals or groups praying together) promotes social interaction, which is a characteristic of the outward movement of prayer. This holy act is often done in a group setting where people come together and share prayer requests and concerns. Afterwards, people will pray and seek God's face. Bible studies and small prayer groups are a couple of examples of people aggregating and inspiring and encouraging one another. Small group prayer sessions also help people deal with issues collectively. There have been times where I participated in a small group, and a member made a serious prayer request that literally forced the group to pray over the person and offer words of affirmation and support. In one small group, I remember a lady disclosing to the group that she was sexually abused, and we prayed over her, demonstrating the outward movement of prayer.

Acts 6 demonstrates that prayer sometimes involves social interaction. In this story, the apostles laid their hands on the seven converts and prayed for them to walk in their calling. The very act of coming to the apostles and receiving prayer is social interaction because power was transferred from the apostles onto those for whom they prayed. As a result, the Disciples of Christ grew in number. Through this act, the people were affirmed and validated in their call to ministry. Now, this experience couldn't occur in a vacuum, but in a community. These seven converts could have stayed home and prayed for themselves, but they would not have received the same power from God that they received the day the apostles laid their hands on them. We see that God impacts communities through prayer.

In addition, as believers in Christ, one way that we experience God is through corporate prayer. For the record, corporate prayer is seen more in the books following the Gospels and even throughout the Psalter. Some of the prayers in Psalms were sung by temple worshipers.

Corporate prayer is witnessed elsewhere in the Book of Acts, which introduces us to the formation of the Christian church and stresses the importance of corporate prayer. Acts 1:14 says, "They all joined together constantly in prayer, along with the women and Mary the mother of Jesus, and with his brothers." Though their prayer is not recorded, it appears that they prayed for the replacement for Judas as an apostle. The Scripture strongly encourages us to pray with others in Acts 2:42-43: "They devoted themselves to the apostles' teaching and to fellowship, to the breaking of bread and to prayer. Everyone was filled with awe at the many wonders and signs performed by the apostles." This account paints the picture of corporate prayer.

Another aspect of corporate prayer that I want to point out is that communal empowerment may take place through prayer. Looking at the two verses from Acts 2 reveal that after the prayer, the believers in Christ performed miracles. This means they were able to help people that they encountered who were in need.

My former pastor and mentor stressed that all the church members pray together prior to the beginning of service. As a result of his request, we would go in the choir loft of the church and pray for about a half hour before the service. This prayer set the tone for the service as we focused on worshiping God.

Corporate prayer highlights a communal experience of God. If we take a closer look at the above example in Acts, we notice that the Early Church encountered the living presence of God. They were able to select Matthias as the replacement for Judas. This prayer represents unity and oneness.

Notice the wonders and signs that took place after the apostles devoted themselves to prayer. They had to be on the same page with their prayer lives to accomplish the things that God intended. The apostles had to walk in step with the plan of God revealed in prayer. It is as if God used prayer as the prerequisite for the miraculous events that would soon follow in the lives of the apostles (Acts 3:1-16, 9:33-35, and 16:6-8). Prayer taps into the senses of God and makes the miraculous possible.

To summarize, corporate prayer is a necessity for the church. Just like in the text, prayer set the spiritual tone for the churches in the region where the book of Acts was written. It will do the same thing for us today. We should pray as congregations. We should pray as families. We should pray as small groups. God will use this medium of prayer to empower communities and make a positive difference in the world.

EXERCISE

There is scientific research that shows that exercise can reduce stress and enhance one's mental, physical, and emotional health. "Cardiovascular exercises such as biking, swimming and walking are helpful because one is able to greatly increase blood circulation to the brain and manage one's mood."[22] Heart health makes a major tangible difference in one's life. What the study highlights is that when one is done exercising; one is in a better mood and can better deal with stress or depression.[23]

Prayer is an exercise of faith. Specifically, we exercise that which is in our heart. Each time someone prays, they build up their faith muscles, which help in times of prosperity and adversity. Through this exercise, they rely on the sustaining hand of God to take them through whatever life brings. Through prayer in faith, we walk toward God. In Exodus 20, the prophet Moses walked up Mount Sinai to receive the Ten Commandments

---
22 Stibich, Mark. https://www.verywellmind.com/exercise-and-improving-your-mood-2223781 wirttien on August 13, 2019 (accessed on December 15, 2019).
23 Bassio, Julia C. and Suzuki, Wendy A. *The Effects of Acute Exercise on Mood, Cognition Neurophysiology and Neurochemical Pathways: A Review.* March 28, 2017 (accessed on December 15, 2019).

and pray. He had an intense conversation with the living God. Moses' action demonstrates the spiritual exercise of walking toward the Divine, which is associated with prayer.

Through prayer, God heals the mind and body. The scientific studies only reinforce what the Bible teaches us about the power of God through prayer. God calms our minds and strengthens our bodies. Stressors become alleviated through prayer. We should continue to pray and seek God's face.

TRANSFORMATION

When it comes to the relationship between prayer and transformation, God doesn't change, but the hearts and actions of humans do. This point is reiterated throughout Scripture. In Acts 9:4-6, we find the words to Saul's prayer which lead to a complete one-eighty. "He fell to the ground and heard a voice say to him, 'Saul, Saul, why do you persecute me?' "Who are you, Lord?" Saul asked. 'I am Jesus, whom you are persecuting,' he replied. 'Now get up and go into the city, and you will be told what you must do.'" Prior to this prayer, Saul was the notorious killer of many Christians; he was on a mission to kill Christians in Damascus (Acts 7). He terrorized the Christian church (Acts 8:3) and was responsible for the death of Stephen (Acts 8:1-2), the first Christian martyr. By Acts 9, God stopped Paul dead in his tracks and conversed with him.

During this conversation, Paul experienced conversion and, through the power of the Spirit of God, decided to share the Gospel in Asia Minor and Europe with the Gentiles. The evidence of Paul's change manifested itself when the scales fell off his eyes and he received the vision of the Lord to preach the Gospel. The whole course of Paul's life changed through prayer because God elevated Paul's level of consciousness so that he became aware of God's plan and purpose for his life. Not only did Paul receive this awesome revelation; but as the Scripture informs us, Paul also walked in his calling.

Following the prayer, he even went through a name change from Saul to Paul. As Paul, he became one of the greatest evangelists by being a mentor to other Christians, writing between "13 letters of the New Testament" and "establishing many churches."[24] The instrument that God used for this great man of faith was transformational prayer.

God uses prayer as the agent of transformation for personal, emotional, and social change and for the restoration of relationships. Through God, prayer can help us be nicer, calmer, and more considerate human beings. I have observed these types of changes in the lives of people I know. Emotionally, God uses prayer to stabilize moods and emotions. Therefore, prayer guides people to healthy ways of expressing themselves. Through prayer, God gives us peace, tranquility, and a healthy balance in life because we can unify our thoughts with God.

Perhaps, some of us need to be powered on prayer today. We need God to awaken our level of consciousness so that we become aware of God's direction for our lives. Perhaps, some of us are working at dead-end jobs or are in unfulfilling relationships. We need God's power to walk in His purpose for our lives.

In the end, God's power makes a gigantic difference in our lives. The power of God will alert and remind us of the presence of God at work in us. Our consciousness will be opened by the spiritual encounter that we experience in prayer, and we will be able to follow God's will for our lives. Paul became an apostle and left a legacy on the Christian church as a result of being powered on by God. We, too, can impact the earth when we allow God's power to be turned on in our lives.

---

24 Godwin Goziem Jireh, "Which Books of the Bible Did Paul Write and What Make Them Distinct?," Quora.com, https://www.quora.com/Which-books-of-the-Bible-did-Paul-write-and-what-makes-them-distinct (accessed on December 7, 2018).

UPGRADE

We may view the transformation associated by God through prayer through the lens of a cell phone upgrade. Every couple of years, I am eligible for a cell phone upgrade, which means that I can get a newer phone that has more capabilities than my previous phone. This means that my internet connection is faster; the phone screen is wider; the camera on my phone provides a clearer picture. These upgrades speak to the evolution of cell phones.

Just like these mobile devices have evolved over time, so has prayer. Before the internet, churches didn't have prayer chains, prayer text messages, and twenty-four/seven prayer lines. There are also Skype prayer sessions where people can look at each other and pray with each other, even though they are a long distance away. These opportunities enable people to connect with God and each other daily.

CHAPTER 8
LOCKED OUT

"Then I will tell them plainly, 'I never knew you. Away from me, you evildoers!'"
(Matthew 7:23).

Many computers and smartphones are passcode-protected; and if one doesn't enter the password, they are locked out or unable to have access to the computer. These passcodes keep one's data safe. Sometimes, people may make attempts at entering the right passcode to their device and get locked out once they reach three failed attempts.

Another way to understand passcode protection is to think of it as a veil for the computer. In the same way, there may be a lock or a barrier that prohibits prayer from reaching God. These barriers include self-centeredness and a disconnection from God. The obstacles make life difficult.

BARRIERS TO PRAYER

Just like there are barriers that may inhibit people from using their mobile devices, there are a couple barriers that discourage people from praying. These are barriers that have people feeling locked out from the presence of God. Doubt and viewing God as distant are to symptoms of prayerlessness. These two symptoms hinder and dishearten people from prayer.

DOUBT

Doubt is static that hinders our prayers from getting through. It is like having a bad signal, which disrupts communication. James 1:5-7 says, "If any of you lacks wisdom, you should ask God, who gives generously to all without finding fault, and it will be given to you. But when you ask, you must believe and not doubt, because the one who doubts is like a wave of the sea, blown and tossed by the wind. That person should not expect to receive anything from the Lord." This means that we can use our doubts and insecurities to propel us to pray. We should use our human frailties as the reason that we seek God in prayer. This doesn't mean that we should pray not expecting God to act. On the contrary, while praying, we must refuse to believe that God is unable to fix our situation or fix the individual(s) for whom we are praying.

DISTANCE OF GOD

First, some find it is hard to communicate with God because they see God as aloof and distant. Furthermore, some may think that God does not want to have a relationship with humanity. These beliefs are why these individuals do not talk to God at all. Perhaps that is you. You think God is too good to talk to you. Today, I pray that you realize that is not the case at all. In the Old and New Testament, there are many prayers that indicate that God wants to commune with people through prayer.

On the other hand, we find King David saying, "How long, Lord? Will you forget me forever? How long will you hide your face from me" (Psalm 13:1). This prayer means that David felt abandoned by God. From viewing his words, he felt that God wasn't with him during his distress. Yet, he didn't use the fact that he felt that God discarded him as an excuse to not pray. He prayed despite his feelings.

Prayer bridges the gap between humanity and God. We can feel God's energy and presence in our lives during prayer. This sacred act makes God feel close even when conditions in our lives do not change immediately.

These barriers contaminate our prayers. They serve as hindrances to our prayers because we do not operate in faith. Doubt is like noise that distracts us from focusing on the presence and power of God. Through prayer, God is never distant from us though we may feel this way.

PRAYING IN THE SPIRIT

Instead of falling prey to these hindrances; we need to pray in the spirit. There are five references for praying in the Spirit in the New Testament (Ephesians 6:18, Jude 1:20, 1 Corinthiains 14:15, Galatians 5:16-17, and Romans 8:26-27). Praying in the Spirit addresses the issue of not knowing how to pray. Romans 8:26-27 says: "In the same way, the Spirit helps us in our weakness. We do not know what we ought to pray for, but the Spirit himself intercedes for us through wordless groans. And he who searches our hearts knows the mind of the Spirit, because the Spirit intercedes for God's people in accordance with the will of God." This means that our prayers are assisted by the Holy Spirit.

Praying in the spirit is not an emotional activity. This is not spiritual ecstasy. On the other hand, it is the Holy Spirit moving in such a powerful way in our hearts which deepens our desire for God. We hunger and thirst for God like we do food and water.

> "My heart rejoices in the Lord;
> in the Lord my horn is lifted high.
> My mouth boasts over my enemies,
> for I delight in your deliverance.
> "There is no one holy like the Lord;
> there is no one besides you;
> there is no Rock like our God" (1 Samuel 2:1-2).

This prayer is a Spirit-led prayer that highlights her sincerity.

The Holy Spirit takes our requests and perfects them in the presence of the Almighty (Romans 8:26). In other words, praying in the Spirit means that the Holy Spirit reframes and refines the words of our prayers so that God will receive the prayer.

Two more obstacles are insecurity and anxiety. They may have a lock on you which keeps you from experiencing joy. These two vices have a tight grip and have disrupted relationships and put a strain on you, keeping you from enjoying your life. It's time to be set free. How does one get set free? I am so glad that you asked.

God uses prayer to unlock His blessings for our lives. These blessings may come in the form of a sharper focus in life, deliverance, and a positive outlook on life. To experience these blessings, we must push past insecurity and doubt with the help of the Lord.

ENTERING THE CODE

Typically, after a wireless device is on, the user may have to enter a passcode. This code allows the individual to login into their device. Usually, people have passcodes that have sentimental meaning to them. Some use their birth dates, and others use initials from their names. Each passcode is unique to the individual.

A passcode is also used for security reasons to protect devices from being compromised and broken into by unwanted guests. In terms of wireless communication, if one has access to another person's password, he or she can hack into one's email or phone contacts and send messages from their device and even access one's personal pictures on their wireless device. So, a code is necessary when it comes to securing wireless devices.

I equate Elijah's prayer time with God, where he accessed the Lord's heart and moved beyond his personal barriers, to one entering a passcode into wireless device (1 Kings 19:14-20). He was able to move on and fulfill his purpose after he had this encounter with God.

TECHNICAL ISSUES

It is always convenient when wireless communication works. There is nothing like being able to check my email, listen to my voice messages, and surf the internet. However, sometimes devices don't function properly.

One of the common problems that prevent devices from working properly is viruses. Viruses are infections that stop the computer from working and slow down internet speed. Ultimately, this means that viruses derail one from doing any work on his or her computer or device.

Another issue that a virus causes is connectional failure. The other day at work, there was a technical failure that prohibited employees from completing their tasks. As usual, some people complained because they had deadlines that they were not able to meet. The other issue is we didn't know when the connectional issue would be resolved; so, we were stuck in a state of not knowing when we would have access to the internet.

When the software doesn't work properly, electronic companies suggest that the customer call them for technical assistance. Spiritually, a primary technical issue that people have is unbelief. Unbelief will prevent a person from trusting in God.

In the Bible, we learn of a gentleman that had a sick son that he wanted to be healed. He understood that he lacked trust in God. Mark 9:24-25 says, "Immediately the boy's father exclaimed, 'I do believe; help me overcome my unbelief!' When Jesus saw that a crowd was running to the scene, he rebuked the impure spirit. 'You deaf and mute spirit,' he said, 'I command you, come out of him and never enter him again.'" He acknowledged that he needed to have a firm faith foundation.

A third issue is pain. Emotional pain can cause people to speak in haste and make rash decisions. Physical pain can cause people to not think clearly. From the Holy Scriptures, Paul is going through a horrific, but unknown ordeal, so he offers an urgent prayer to the Lord. But the Lord doesn't respond how he expects. Second Corinthians 12:7-10 says:

Or because of these surpassingly great revelations. Therefore, in order to keep me from becoming conceited, I was given a thorn in my flesh, a messenger of Satan, to torment me. Three times I pleaded with the Lord to take it away from me. But he said to me, "My grace is sufficient for you, for my power is made perfect in weakness." Therefore I will boast all the more gladly about my weaknesses, so that Christ's power may rest on me. That is why, for Christ's sake, I delight in weaknesses, in insults, in hardships, in persecutions, in difficulties. For when I am weak, then I am strong.

This is how Paul dealt with his pain.

TECHNICAL SUPPORT

The first question that all technicians ask is what type of device the customer is calling in reference to. The technician needs to know this information so that the technician may determine how to remedy the issue. For example, the approach to repairing a cell phone isn't the same course of action that would be needed for a computer. Besides, each device has its own unique composition. So, a technical approach is needed to solve the problem.

Through God, prayer gives us the technical support needed through life. We have the assurance that we never walk alone in life. We never face the troubles of life alone.

In Isaiah 58, the author writes to the Israelites informing them that they need technical support. They needed support to respect the Sabbath and turn away from sin (Isaiah 58:13). Exploitation of the poor and unwholesome talk were key issues at the time and were common issues for the time. Isaiah 58:9: "If you do away with the yoke of oppression, with the pointing finger and malicious talk." This behavior put the people at odds with God.

DIAGNOSE THE PROBLEM

After the technician is aware of the type of device, he or she is going to diagnose the problem by completing a diagnostic test. A diagnostic test helps determine why the computer is running slow or why the internet is not working on the device. Following the diagnostic test, the technician can determine a solution.

Psalm 139 paints the picture of God diagnosing a problem. Psalm 139:1-4 says:
> You have searched me, LORD,
> and you know me.
> You know when I sit and when I rise;
> you perceive my thoughts from afar.
> You discern my going out and my lying down;
> you are familiar with all my ways.
> Before a word is on my tongue
> you, Lord, know it completely.

These words reveal that God knows all about us, which means that God knows our deficiencies and mistakes.

THE PRAYER OPERATION

Prayer is a human-to-Divine operation. As the Operator, God works on our behalf, and the system that God operates is our lives. We come to God, who is the Master Operator, and ask for His assistance in guiding and transforming our lives. God is the One Who operates when we wake up by giving us breath in our bodies and a sound mind. God demonstrates His role as Operator by giving us traveling mercies to different destinations.

Through our prayers and God's faithfulness, we receive energy and strength for the tasks that lie ahead. Romans 15:5 says, "May the God who gives endurance and encouragement give you the same attitude of mind toward each other that Christ Jesus had." Additionally, prayer gives us strategies to deal with the trials and tribulations that life throws our way. Philippians 4:6-7 says, "Do not be anxious about anything, but in every situation, by prayer and petition, with thanksgiving, present your requests to God. And the peace of God, which transcends all understanding, will guard your hearts and your minds in Christ Jesus."

THE MASTER TECHNICIAN

Let's look at the Master Technician at work. Mark 5:21-24, 35-43 gives an account of Jairus, a synagogue leader who asked that Jesus heal his daughter. Prior to Jesus arriving at the home of Jairus' daughter, he was sidetracked by another situation (the healing of the woman with the issue of blood). After Jesus healed the woman with the issue of blood (Mark 5:24-34), people from Jairus' house labeled his request for help as a lost cause because they assumed that his daughter was dead. Jesus, being the Master Technician, observed the girl Himself and determined that she was asleep and not dead. He told her to get up, and she arose. He also told her parents that she needed something to eat.

See, Jesus intercedes on our behalf and gets to the root of our problems. He detects the problem and gives us the solution. These solutions result in a renewed body and renewed relationships. Though not stated in the Bible, I believe that Jairus and his daughter may have grown closer after this ordeal. Jesus may have brought this family closer together.

An additional virus that can hinder our prayer time is our very active human brain, sometimes called "monkey-brain" because it jumps from one thought to another in its search for stimulation or potential threats. This proclivity to be easily distracted can keep us from operating efficiently. The regular practice of prayer can increase our capacity to focus, thereby developing our problem-solving skills. Prayer is what allows us to operate efficiently as people because it strengthens, sustains, and stimulates us.

Finally, prayer is a way to help us navigate through this journey of life. Through the lens of technological support, we may view God's work in our lives through prayer. Like a Technician, God works in our lives through prayer.

CHAPTER 9

BUILDING A STRONGER NETWORK

"I urge, then, first of all, that petitions, prayers, intercession and thanksgiving be made for all people" (1 Timothy 2:1).

All mobile providers want to be the largest network carrier. This is a fancy way of saying that one company has more subscribers than another company. Currently, Verizon Wireless takes the crown as the largest wireless network in America. "Verizon has 145.743 million subscribers across the United States."[25] Unlimited data plans and faster internet connections are things that set Verizon apart.

Interestingly with wireless communication, some of the subscribers mentioned left the network and returned for one reason or another. Perhaps, the subscriber sought to pay less for another network, but was dissatisfied with the service that he or she received. In the end, the subscriber returned to the network.

When it comes to prayer, there can always be more people added to this network. The truth is that everybody needs prayers offered on their behalf. What I am referring to is known as intercessory prayer. Intercessory prayer means standing in the gap for another person.

---

25 Mike Dano, "How Verizon, AT&T, T-Mobile, Spring, and More Stacked Up in Q4 2016: The Top 7 Carriers," FierceWireless.com, http://www.fiercewireless.com/wireless/how-verizon-at-t-t-mobile-sprint-and-more-stacked-up-q4-2016-top-7-carriers (accessed August 5, 2017).

OUTWARD MOVEMENT

Intercessory prayer has more broadest coverage area than any mobile network provider. Think about it: prayer even impacts people who don't have access to wireless communication. People who don't have cell phones, laptops, or iPads may still experience the power of God through prayer. In fact, building a stronger network can be seen through praying for others. This type of praying for others changes dynamics and situations. Why should we pray for others? The reason is because we are called to intercessory prayer. Hebrews 13:18 says, "Pray for us." We are sure that we have a clear conscience and desire to live honorably in every way.

Intercessory prayer was common during biblical times. With the pages of the Old Testament, the prophets of Israel prayed for those in the ancient world (Genesis 18:16-32 and Deuteronomy 9:26). In these instances, Abraham and Moses, pleaded with God to spare the people of Sodom and the Israelites from destruction. Additionally, we see intercessory prayer in the New Testament. While on Earth, Jesus prayed for his disciples. To speak about Jesus' profound prayers in a twenty-first century context, we may view His prayers as Jesus entering a code and having unlimited access to the heart of God.

One such prayer is shown in John 17. Jesus enters His petition to God to express His desire for Christian unity. Jesus utters this prayer, requesting unity among the believers and the world. There was a brewing theological tension between the Jews and Christians which caused separation at the time of this passage. Considering this strain, we find this powerful prayer.

> My prayer is not for them alone. I pray also for those who will believe in me through their message, that all of them may be one, Father, just as you are in me and I am in you. May they also be in us so that the world may believe that you have sent me. I have given them the glory that you gave me, that they may be one as we are one—I in them and you in me—so that they may be brought to complete unity. Then the world will know that you sent me and have loved them even as you have loved me (John 17:20-24).

Jesus illustrates unity by using the example of the closeness between Him and God to underscore that the disciples needed to be unified. He wanted his disciples to walk in unity and togetherness with Him. This spirit of unity would prepare the believers for the upcoming persecution they would face following the death of Christ (John 20).

Intercessory prayer is unselfish prayer. In other words, it means caring about the feelings, emotions and situations of others. This form of prayer is practiced in the Old Testament book of Job. Job 42:10 informs us that Job's fortunes were restored after he prayed for his friends. He lost his family and property; and finally, he prayed for his buddies and received everything back. It appears that his situation drastically improved when he prayed earnestly for his friends.

We can view Earth as a network, and we must view prayer as the medium to upgrade the network (education, clean energy, environment, and economy) around us. James 1:5 says, "If any of you lacks wisdom, you should ask God, who gives generously to all without finding fault, and it will be given to you." Wisdom is needed to address the issues, and we must ask for it.

INTERCESSORY PRAYER

From reading and analyzing Jesus' prayer of intercession in John 17, there are two goals of intercessory prayer: oneness and unity. John 17:21 says, "That all of them may be one, Father, just as you are in me and I am in you. May they also be in us so that the world may believe that you have sent me." Oneness highlights that God the Father and God the Son have an inseparable connection.

As it comes to prayer, we should pray that our lives mimic the oneness and union of God the Father and God the Son. Our prayer may help our congregation to be one and to reflect the love and togetherness that you have with your son.

John 17:23 illustrates unity in mission and purpose. "I in them and you in me—so that they may be brought to complete unity. Then the world will know that you sent me and have loved them even as you have loved me." Unity is when people come together to fulfill a certain purpose.

This type of prayer centers on focusing on the mission of the church, which is spreading the Gospel. We should pray that members of the universal church of Jesus Christ implement effective strategies to spread the love of God. This should be our prayer.

Oneness and unity should be ingredients of our prayers of intercession. We should pray that the church of Jesus Christ will greatly focus on sharing the Gospel message of Jesus Christ. This should be our primary prayer of intercession.

RECONCILIATION

Another goal of intercessory prayer revealed in the Scriptures is reconciliation. Reconciliation means restoring relationships. Look at Paul's conversion prayer, which reconciled Paul and God. Prior to this prayer, Paul was not a Christian. In fact, Paul, then known as Saul, terrorized the Christian church (Acts 8:3). His goal was to rid the land of Christians. Following Paul's prayer on the road to Damascus, he came into a relationship with God. He shared the Gospel message (Acts 1:8) and encouraged giving to the poor (Acts 20:1-15).

One moral of Paul's story is that radical reconciliation is achievable through time with God in prayer. The Lord forgave Paul and opened the door for a continued relationship. The good news from this passage is that our broken relationships can be restored. This means that it is time to let go of all the grudges that you are holding on to.

The Creator uses prayer as the pipeline that changes people. Therefore, we should continue to take the time to pray for other people so that relationships are restored. Continue to pray and watch God's work in your personal life, communities, and the world.

We must understand that intercessory prayer is a major responsibility. We should take the time to pray for others each day. This is a sign of care and concern for other individuals. In the end, we find that intercessory prayer is an unselfish act of worship.

The Scriptures contain many prayers that we may repeat and incorporate into our personal and intercessory prayer time. There are just five biblical prayers found in Scripture that resulted in a move from God. There are themes and Scriptures aimed to guide you in your time of prayer. I strongly urge you to pray these prayers, and you should expect a torrential down-pouring of Divine activity and blessings in your life and the lives of others. Here are some prayers that we may recite and use to pray for others.

PRAYER #1: HOLY LIVING

"May he strengthen your hearts so that you will be blameless and holy in the presence of our God and Father when our Lord Jesus comes with all his holy ones" (1 Thessalonians 3:13).

Do you want to live a life pleasing in God's sight? Holy living is the way to do so. Psalm 51:10 is a prayer that gives voice to holy living in this way: "Create in me a pure heart, O God, and renew a steadfast spirit within me." This is a prayer that we should say before we get into the activity of our day. It prepares us for the decisions and challenges that we will face. From personal experience, I guarantee that God will transform and reshape outcomes in life. Look what it did for King David. Throughout the Psalms, we read how he united the northern and southern kingdom.

Holy living will help us awaken the Divine within us. We can activate kindness, patience, and love as the fruits of prayer. We can follow God through holy living with constant communication in prayer.

It is also important to note that holy living also enables to us to live in the confidence that we are living a life that is according to God's will. We don't have to go through life wondering if our actions are aligned with how God wants us to live. Instead, we go through life with assurance that our decisions are right in tune with God's expectations.

Another aspect of holy living that often goes unmentioned is advocating for the needs of the marginalized. The marginalized include the poor and those who face discrimination. Further, this means being a voice for the voiceless. We find the example of God empowering Moses through prayer to be the voice of the enslaved Israelites in the Old Testament when he spoke to Pharaoh demanding freedom in Exodus 7:2. In this instance, Moses fought against the injustices, which stood in line with God's plan for the people of Israel.

One of our fervent prayers should be that we are agents of social justice in the world for those left behind. The left behind are those who are abused, those who are discriminated against, those who are mistreated, and those who are ostracized, such as the poor, orphans and the widows—just to name a few (Luke 14:13 and James 1:27). We should be willing to adopt the compliant posture that Moses did when he accepted God's assignment and became the leader who would help liberate the Jewish people from Egyptian captivity.

We may say, "Lord, help me to meet the needs of the marginalized. Provide me with opportunities to help those in need. Help me to show compassion to those less fortunate." This prayer personifies holy living.

PRAYER #2: OVERCOMING

"God is our refuge and strength, an ever-present help in trouble" (Psalm 46:1).

Hardships are part of the journey of life. Sometimes, we may experienc bumps and twists in our days on Earth. However, we should not throw in th towel when things get rough. Therefore, the only choice we have is to trust i

God and overcome our obstacles. Overcoming is the encouragement needed to make it through difficulty and to persevere through adversity.

A worried father in the New Testament asked Jesus for the power to overcome doubt. This account from Mark 9:14-24 is about the father who prayed for the healing of his son and for stronger faith in the Lord. Let's look at this sample prayer for overcoming doubt: "I do believe; help me overcome my unbelief" (Mark 9:24). This man prayed for faith during troubling circumstances. Digging deeper, it appears that this man wanted to overcome doubt because he distanced himself from God every time something negative happened in his life.

In times of doubt, we can pray this prayer and expect God to act. In the following verse, Jesus "rebuked the impure spirit." Jesus recognized this man's plea for faith and healed him.

Like the sick man in the passage, Jesus also hears our cries for help. It is as if God extends His hand toward us to not only lift us up, but also to help us overcome. It is God's plan that we overcome in life.

PRAYER #3: UNIVERSAL IMPACT

"I urge, then, first of all, that petitions, prayers, intercession and thanksgiving be made for all people" (1 Timothy 2:1).

Pray the Prayer of Jabez for restoration and for unity in the country and throughout the world: "Jabez was more honorable than his brothers. His mother had named him Jabez, saying, 'I gave birth to him in pain.' Jabez cried out to the God of Israel, 'Oh, that you would bless me and enlarge my territory! Let your hand be with me, and keep me from harm so that I will be free from pain.' And God granted his request" (1 Chronicles 4:9-10). This meant that the Lord allowed his petition to come into being.

The impact of this prayer is felt in the succeeding verses. First, we take note that Jabez's influence greatly increased, and the land prospered. This meant that things were improving for Jabez.

We should ask that God enlarge our territory of influence. We should ask that God send people our way that we may minister to. These may be family members, neighbors, co-workers, friends, or even strangers. We should ask how we may serve these people.

Like Jabez, this prayer will have a universal impact on our lives. Our lives will change in the way that God desires. This is the universal impact that God offers through prayer.

PRAYER #4: RENEWED MIND

> *"Do not conform to the pattern of this world, but be transformed by the renewing of your mind"* (Romans 12:2).

A renewed mind means that we are restored and refreshed. We need a mind that is restored so that we may process what God wants us to do. Looking through the Bible, we find an example of someone who prayed for a renewed mind.

In Psalm 60, we encounter a victorious David in battle over the Edomites (Psalm 60:8). We learn in 2 Samuel 5:19 that David, a man of prayer, had a renewed mind and received direction from God as to how he should attack the Philistines.

A renewed mind will energize and invigorate us to serve God and fulfill our Divine purpose. Following David's example, we will be able to understand God's will and how to operate in God's will after we pray.

Think of this renewed mind like a system restore. The system restore may take our mobile device back to a previous time when our system functioned properly. A renewed mind is the restoration of our mind. We can have a clear mind with the absence of regrets and fears.

For a renewed mind, pray these words: "May these words of my mouth and this mediation of my heart be pleasing in your sight, LORD, my Rock and my Redeemer" (Psalm 19:14).

PRAYER #5: PEACE

*"The L*ORD *gives strength to his people; the L*ORD *blesses his people with peace"* (Psalm 29:11).

Stress and anxiety threaten our peace. When we feel overwhelmed by the troubles of life, we may pray Psalm 3:1-6:

> Lord, how many are my foes! How many rise up against me! Many are saying of me, "God will not deliver him." But you, LORD, are a shield around me, my glory, the One who lifts my head high. I call out to the LORD, and he answers me from his holy mountain. I lie down and sleep; I wake again, because the Lord sustains me. I will not fear though tens of thousands assail me on every side. Arise, LORD! Deliver me, my God!

In Psalm 4:8, David praises God that he can sleep in peace. Through prayer, God pours peace into our lives. The waters of peace will wash us and ease tensions. Peace will permeate our lives and help us to relax in times of stress. Are you ready to receive peace today?

All these prayers are significant and made a difference in the life of the one making the petition. Families and lives were transformed and restored because of the prayers of faith offered by these biblical heroes. All of these biblical characters had their share of faults and failures but did not allow their shortcomings to keep them from praying.

LOGGING OFF

"For no matter how many promises God has made, they are 'Yes' in Christ. And so through him the 'Amen' is spoken by us to the glory of God" (2 Corinthians 1:20).

Logging off is a process that pertains to the session end on a computer, an email account, and social media accounts. In terms of email, this is another way of closing a session or an account. When it comes to logging off an email account, it means that one will not be able to access their email without logging back on.

A benefit of logging off is that an individual doesn't have to shut down the computer. This is a faster option than restarting a computer. With email or social media, it is easier to log back onto our accounts by just simply entering our password.

AMEN

Saying amen is how we log off prayer. It is the closing statement of prayer. *Amen* is the word people use to end a prayer, and it means "let it be so." This means to let it come to pass, and it is a way of releasing our prayer unto God.

CONCLUSION

Wireless communication continues to dominate our culture. We love to stay connected to people wherever we are. With what has been reviewed throughout this work, I hope people will stay connected with God through prayer. We can maximize time here on Earth and spend it in prayer. Through God, prayer shapes, strengthens, and shakes us at times, which will help us grow. Prayer nourishes us to grow in our relationship with our Maker. It will help us to know God and God's expectations in our lives.

In closing, prayer is the vehicle in which we communicate with God. We are able to reach out to the Lord and commune with our Creator. A connection is established and is daily rekindled through prayer. Prayer is meaningful and effective. Hopefully, the information in this book is helpful as you grow in your walk with the Lord.

I hope that *Prayer: The Most Reliable Wireless Communication* has informed and encouraged you to pursue God in prayer. Hopefully, you now have a lasting visual of the power of God through prayer that will transform your life. Looking at prayer through the prism of wireless communication intends to bring clarity to this sacred discipline. With a renewed mind, go seek the Lord through prayer.

I sincerely hope that this book served to educate you on the purpose and power of God through prayer in a new and enlightening way. Hopefully, this resource will encourage you to pray. Prayer is the original wireless communication; and unlike today's devices, it is always reliable. The central message of this manuscript is that prayer is a lifestyle. It is a way of living. We must walk and move forward. Through God, prayer changes people, things, and situations. This means that it is not a waste of time and is productive.

PRAYER OF SALVATION

Prayer opens the door for one coming into a relationship with Christ. Just to be clear, prayer is only the initial step for one coming to salvation (Romans 10:9-10). What is also key is to let this prayer come to life through righteous living (James 2:17). Live a life that pleases God (Psalm 19:14).

Dear Lord,

I am a sinner, and I want to invite You to come into my heart and life as my Savior. I ask for the forgiveness of my sins today. I truly want a relationship with You, Jesus Christ. Have your way with me. In Jesus' Name, I pray. Amen.

PRAYER OF BLESSING

Dear Lord,

I pray that this book blesses everyone who reads it in a special way. I pray that a revival of prayer will manifest on the Earth. Help people to pray for their neighbors and family members. Draw us closer to you, Lord Jesus Christ. Move in us. We pray in Jesus' Name. Amen!

I welcome your feedback. Please drop me a line and tell me how this book has blessed your life.

If you are ever in the Baltimore area, please join us for worship at 11:00 a.m. at Mt. Zion United Methodist Church, located at 3800 Black Rock Road Upperco, MD 21155.

AFTERWORD

Reader, I sincerely hope that you are encouraged to seek God in prayer. Prayer is the most productive and fulfilling discipline that we can practice. When we connect with God through prayer, power, restoration, and transformation will take permanent residence in our lives.

A CALL TO PRAY

I strongly encourage you to join a prayer group at church. Start a Skype prayer session with people who you are familiar with. Perhaps, God is tugging at your heart strings, urging you to begin a prayer group. If so, it's time to establish this ministry in your church.

BIBLIOGRAPHY

Banco, Erin. "FBI Director Christopher Wray Says Russia Remains a Threat to 2020 Election," TheDailyBeast.com. https://www.thedailybeast.com/fbi-director-christopher-wray-says-russia-remains-a-threat-to-2020-election. (accessed on April 27, 2019).

Bassio, Julia C. and Suzuki, Wendy A. *The Effects of Acute Exercise on Mood, Cognition, Neurophysiology and Neurochemical Pathways: A Review.* March 28, 2017. (accessed on December 15, 2019).

Bertolucci, Jeff. "*Six Things That Block Your WiFi, and How to Fix Them* May 16, 2011." https://www.pcworld.com/article/227973/six_things_that_block_your_wifi_and_how_to_fix_them.html?page=2. (accessed May 29, 2019).

Bhumi Suktam, Atharva. "*Prayer to Mother Earth for Grace*" Veda xii.1.3 Source: Hindu Declaration on Climate Change. (accessed August 5, 2018).

Bible Hub, s.v. "*proseuchomai,*" http://biblehub.com/greek/4336.htm. (accessed June 4, 2018).

CNN Library. "*Hinduism Fast Facts*" https://www.cnn.com/2013/11/07/world/hinduism-fast-facts/index.html Published on August 28, 2018. (accessed August 7, 2019).

Dano, Mike. "*How Verizon, AT&T, T-Mobile, Spring, and More Stacked Up in Q4 2016: The Top 7 Carriers.*" FierceWireless.com. http://www.fiercewireless.com/

wireless/how-verizon-at-t-t-mobile-sprint-and-more-stacked-up-q4-2016-top-7-carriers. (accessed August 5, 2017).

Dictionary.com. s.v. "introspection." https://www.dictionary.com/browse/introspection. (accessed December 6, 2018).

"Factors Affecting Wireless Network Performance." *4GonSolutions.com.* http://www.4gon.co.uk/solutions/technical_factors_affecting_wireless_performance.php. (accessed September 8, 2016).

Foster, Richard. *Prayer: The Hearts True Home* (San Francisco, CA: Harper One, 2002). p. 85.

"Getting Prayer." *HealingMission.org.* https://www.healingmission.org/getting-prayer.html. (accessed August 18, 2018).

Jayaram V. "A Few Thoughts About Prayers in Hinduism," *HinduWebsite.com,* https://www.hinduwebsite.com/ask/how-to-pray.asp

Jireh, Godwin Goziem. Quora.com. www.quora.com/Which-books-of-the-Bible-did-Paul-write-and-what-makes-them-distinct (accessed December 7, 2018).

Keller, Timothy. *"Prayer: Experiencing Awe and Intimacy with God"* (New York, NY: Penguin Books, 2014), p. 45.

King, Hope. *"Verizon Now Charges $10 a Day for International Roaming."* Published on November 12, 2015. www.money.cnn.com/2015/11/12/technology/verizon-travelpass. (accessed September 10, 2017).

King, Martin L., Jr. "I Have a Dream." Speech. Lincoln Memorial, Washington, D. C. 28 August 1963. American Rhetoric. Web. (accessed on August 6, 2019).

Littlefair, Sam. *"Do Buddhists Pray? What For?" Lions Roar.com.* www.lionsroar.com/what-is-prayer-in-buddhism. (accessed August 16, 2017).

Schaff, Philip, ed. *Nicene and Post-Nicene Fathers:* First Series S014. Vol. 1. Christian Classics Ethereal Library (Peabody, MA: Hendrickson Pub, 1887), pp. 997-1015.

Schiffman, Richard. *"Why People Who Pray Are Healthier Than Those Who Don't."* HuffingtonPost.com. http://www.huffingtonpost.com/richard-schiffman/why-people-who-pray-are-heathier_b_1197313.html. (accessed September 17, 2016).

"Seasonal Affective Disorder." https://www.mayoclinic.org/diseases-conditions/seasonal-affective-disorder/symptoms-causes/syc-20364651. (accessed May 29, 2019).

"Shout." Crisistextline. https://www.crisistextline.uk (accessed July 12, 2019).

Smith, Melinda M.A. and Segal, Jeanne Ph.D. https://www.helpguide.org/articles/bipolar-disorder/bipolar-disorder-signs-and-symptoms.htm. (accessed May 30, 2019).

Stibich, Mark. https://www.verywellmind.com/exercise-and-improving-your-mood-2223781 written on August 13, 2019. (accessed on December 15, 2019).

Whitsett, Rev. Linda-Martella. https://www.youtube.com/watch?v=DM8fw2nb7ek. (accessed September 27, 2017).

ACKNOWLEDGMENTS

First, I want to give honor to my Lord and Savior Jesus Christ. The Lord guided and directed me through this writing process.

Without the support of my wife, Kirstyn, this great book ministry would not be possible.

Thanks to my parents, brother, and family for their continued support.

Thanks to my publisher, Ambassador International, who made my dream of publishing this work a reality.

Thanks to my Baltimore City Department of Social Services family.

Thanks to all my friends who supported me during the journey completing this book!

For more information about
Rev. John Clark Mayden, Jr.
and
Prayer: The Most Reliable Wireless Communication
connect:

www.facebook.com/john.j.mayden
@jmayden1
Breakingthebarriers82@gmail.com

For more information about
AMBASSADOR INTERNATIONAL
connect:

www.ambassador-international.com
@AmbassadorIntl
www.facebook.com/AmbassadorIntl

If you enjoyed this book, please consider leaving us a review on Amazon, Goodreads, or our website.

More from Ambassador International

This spiritually-inspired memoir argues that, even during the worst of times, maintaining faith can ensure that our best days lie ahead. Victimization presents opportunity for victory, but with God all things are possible because He is the essence of faith.

From Victim to Victor: Walking By Faith and Not By Sight

by Dr. Deandre Collier

Five Minutes to Impact: The Final Flight of the Comanche is a true story of overcoming fear in the face of unexpected crisis, understanding the providence of God in the dealings of man, and renewing our faith in His divine plan for our lives.

Five Minutes to Impact

by David F. Osborne

One Step at a Time is a story of love, faith, family, and friendship, that shows that life isn't easy—it becomes what you make it. God truly can help anyone going through the worst case scenario, you just have to take it one step at a time.

One Step at a Time

by Brian Peahuff

www.ingramcontent.com/pod-product-compliance
Lightning Source LLC
LaVergne TN
LVHW051524070426
835507LV00023B/3291